ITALIAN COOKERY

Boots COOKSHOP
ITALIAN COOKERY

Front cover photograph by Dave Jordan
shows pizza topped with tomatoes, mushrooms,
mozzarella, anchovies and olives (page 35)

Published 1986 on behalf of
The Boots Company Plc, Nottingham, England
by Hamlyn Publishing
Bridge House, London Road, Twickenham,
Middlesex, England

ISBN 0 600 32611 X

Set in Monophoto Gill Sans
by Servis Filmsetting Ltd, Manchester

Printed in Italy

Contents

Useful Facts & Figures

Notes on metrication

In this book quantities are given in metric and Imperial measures. Exact conversion from Imperial to metric measures does not usually give very convenient working quantities and so the metric measures have been rounded off into units of 25 grams. The table below shows the recommended equivalents.

Ounces	Approx g to nearest whole figure	Recommended conversion to nearest unit of 25
1	28	25
2	57	50
3	85	75
4	113	100
5	142	150
6	170	175
7	198	200
8	227	225
9	255	250
10	283	275
11	312	300
12	340	350
13	368	375
14	396	400
15	425	425
16 (1 lb)	454	450
17	482	475
18	510	500
19	539	550
20 (1¼ lb)	567	575

Note When converting quantities over 20 oz first add the appropriate figures in the centre column, then adjust to the nearest unit of 25. As a general guide, 1 kg (1000 g) equals 2.2 lb or about 2 lb 3 oz. This method of conversion gives good results in nearly all cases, although in certain pastry and cake recipes a more accurate conversion is necessary to produce a balanced recipe.

Liquid measures The millilitre has been used in this book and the following table gives a few examples.

Imperial	Approx ml to nearest whole figure	Recommended ml
¼ pint	142	150 ml
½ pint	283	300 ml
¾ pint	425	450 ml
1 pint	567	600 ml
1½ pints	851	900 ml
1¾ pints	992	1000 ml (1 litre)

Spoon measures All spoon measures given in this book are level unless otherwise stated.

Can sizes At present, cans are marked with the exact (usually to the nearest whole number) metric equivalent of the Imperial weight of the contents, so we have followed this practice when giving can sizes.

Oven temperatures

The table below gives recommended equivalents.

	°C	°F	Gas
Very cool	110	225	¼
	120	250	½
Cool	140	275	1
	150	300	2
Moderate	160	325	3
	180	350	4
Moderately hot	190	375	5
	200	400	6
Hot	220	425	7
	230	450	8
Very hot	240	475	9

Note *When making any of the recipes in this book, only follow one set of measures as they are not interchangeable.*

Introduction

There are deep and basic differences between the provinces within Italy, far more than in most other countries of the world. But in diversity is strength. It is precisely because it rests on such distinct traditions that the Italian cuisine is among the finest in the world.

The stereotype of an Italian meal as understood outside Italy would lay heavy stress on spaghetti, olive oil and tomatoes. But spaghetti is only one of the countless different types of pasta, many of which are now commonly available in supermarkets as well as from delicatessens. Nor is the pasta family, with all its ramifications, anything like the only source of carbohydrate on the Italian table. In the northern provinces, its place is usurped by rice and corn meal. Bread is a staple food throughout the country.

As for olive oil, Italy produces great quantities of wonderful, fruity oil, perhaps better even than the oil produced in other countries, and it is basic to much of the cooking in the southernmost areas and the far north. Great quantities of butter are also used and the Milanese cuisine is almost dependant upon it.

Tomatoes are much used in delectable soups, salads and sauces. Other vegetables such as artichokes, beans, beetroot (including the leaves), broccoli, cucumbers, courgettes, mushrooms, peas and sweet peppers are used fresh and in quantity. The Italian housewife thinks nothing of shopping two or even three times a day to catch consignments from the local market gardens as soon as they arrive in the market to make sure they are really fresh and of the best quality.

In the chapters which follow you will find that the recipes are all designed to be within the scope of the non-Italian kitchen. In most cases you will have no difficulty in obtaining all the ingredients and where there is any doubt you will find alternative suggestions. The following brief glossary of authentic ingredients may be of some help in selecting the best ingredients and in identifying the more unusual items.

Alkermes

A crimson red and very sweet cordial prepared from nutmeg, cinnamon, cloves and bay leaves. Coloured with kermes which is an ancient food colouring produced from the dried bodies of insects.

Cheeses

Bel Paese A famous, soft cheese from Lombardy. Widely available and a good addition to any cheeseboard.

Cacio (cacio a cavallo) Made for centuries in the province of Sorrento but also produced in Abruzzi and Apulia, this cheese can be made from whole or skimmed cow's milk. It is a slightly salty, firm cheese shaped like a gourd and hung in pairs.

Caciotta (or caciotto) This is a semi-hard cheese which is made from a mixture of cow's and sheep's milk, from goat's milk or from sheep's milk alone. Cylindrical in shape.

Fontina This is a rich, creamy semi-soft cheese which has some small holes in it, similar to Gruyère. Traditionally, it is used to make *fonduta* which is a dish of melted fontina similar to a fondue.

Mozzarella This is a mild, slightly rubbery cheese made from cow's milk or water buffalo milk. Stored in water, the cheese is used for cooking and particularly for topping pizza.

Parmesan This is probably the most famous Italian cheese. A very hard, strong cheese which can be kept for years and which should be at least two years old. Buy it in chunks to grate yourself (you will need a special grater or use a food processor) or buy it freshly grated from a good delicatessen. The grated cheese can be frozen for several months to be used straight from the freezer as required. Used in cooking and served with pasta dishes or soups.

Pecorino This is the name given to all cheeses made from sheep's milk. The original is *pecorino romano*. This is a hard cheese with a strong flavour, available from delicatessens. Grated and used in cooking.

Reggiano Although Parma gives its name to Parmesan cheese, this type of cheese is also produced in several other places. Reggiano cheese is a Parmesan from Reggio. If it is not available, then substitute any Parmesan.

Ricotta A soft cheese made from sheep's milk. It is creamy and unsalted and available from good supermarkets as well as delicatessens and continental food shops.

Dried Mushrooms

Known as *porcini*, these are available from Italian delicatessens. Pale fawn in colour with a distinctive flavour. If they are brown they are stale and should be avoided. Soak for 15 minutes before use.

Garlic

There is little need to describe this commonly available ingredient. But it is worth noting that plump, fresh bulbs are best. Look out for the red skinned variety and buy a string of garlic in the early autumn if you intend to use a significant quantity in your cooking. Hang it in a cool dry place and it will keep well.

Mortadella

This is a large, smooth pork sausage from Bologna. It is flavoured with white wine and seasoned with spices and whole green peppercorns. Available from supermarkets and delicatessens, the quality varies so it's worth buying the better varieties from a good Italian delicatessen.

Olive Oil

Italy produces several different varieties of olive oil, some probably the best available. Most supermarkets stock at least one type but look in delicatessens for the best quality olive oil. If you use a lot you may find that some Italian delicatessens sell large cans quite reasonably.

Parma Ham

This is smoked ham from Parma. It is eaten raw, cut into slices as fine as tissue paper. Available from good supermarkets and from delicatessens.

Pasta

In Italy fresh pasta is prepared daily for making noodles, baked dishes and stuffed pasta shapes. Fresh pasta dough is not difficult to make, knead and roll by hand. A variety of pasta machines are available and these make the process very easy. The most common, basic machine is used to knead the dough by passing it through widely spaced rollers, then to roll it into sheets and cut it into noodles. Attachments for filling ravioli are also available for such a machine. Electric machines which take the raw ingredients, mix, knead and roll or extrude the pasta dough are also available but they are significantly more expensive and by no means an essential piece of equipment. The following are some of the ways in which fresh pasta dough is used.

Agnolotti Circles of pasta dough stuffed then folded in half and sealed to make semi-circular shapes. They may be stuffed with minced meat and vegetables and served with a meat sauce.

Lasagne The rolled out pasta dough can be cut into wide sheets, boiled and layered with a meat sauce, tomato sauce or cheese and spinach mixture and topped with a creamy sauce or cheese before baking.

Ravioli Small squares of dough filled with meat or spinach and cheese. Served with meat sauce or tomato sauce.

Tagliatelli The rolled out pasta can be cut into ribbon noodles.

Tortellini Small squares of pasta filled with a little meat or spinach mixture and sealed into triangular shape. Two corners of the triangles are pressed together to make a curved shape.

The small stuffed pasta shapes can be served in soups as well as with sauces, herbs and oil or butter and grated Parmesan cheese. Fresh pasta noodles require shorter cooking than dried noodles. About 5 minutes in plenty of boiling salted water is usually enough.

Dried pasta is available in an enormous variety of shapes, from supermarkets as well as delicatessens. Cook dried pasta in plenty of boiling salted water for about 15 minutes, until it is *al dente*, that is tender but with a bit of bite, not oversoft. Drain and serve immediately. The following are some of the types you will find in the shops.

Anellini Very small rings for use in soups.

Cannelloni Large tubes which are boiled, drained and stuffed with meat or vegetable fillings, then coated with sauce and baked.

Conchiglie Shells which can be very small for adding to soups, medium sized or very large. The very large ones are cooked and stuffed.

Farfalle Bow shapes which are served as an accompaniment.

Fettuccine Narrow noodles similar to tagliatelle.

Fusilli Thin spiral shapes of different lengths.

Lasagne Wide strips of pasta, either white or green (coloured and flavoured with spinach).

Macaroni Long pasta tubes, slightly thicker than spaghetti. Also available cut into short pieces, known as short-cut macaroni.

Penne Short quills.

Rigatoni Short, quite wide, ribbed tubes of pasta.

Spaghetti Long thin strands of pasta.

Tagliatelle Ribbon noodles, white or green.

Vermicelli Long fine strands, thinner than spaghetti.

Pine Kernels
The creamy oval kernels of the pine tree. These are quite readily available from delicatessens and health food shops.

Pistachio Nuts
The nut of the pistachio tree, this is pale green in colour with a delicate flavour. Used in both sweet and savoury dishes, available from health food shops, good supermarkets and delicatessens. Also available salted as a snack.

Prosciutto
This is the Italian for raw ham. Parma ham is the best known but others are sold in delicatessens or supermarkets as prosciutto. Cut into very fine slices, often served with melon or figs, also used in cooking.

Salami
Each region – even town – in Italy produces its own variety of salami. Some are fine, others are coarse in texture. Flavoured with herbs and spices, wine and a variety of meats. Most supermarkets offer salami but for the best and most interesting varieties look in Italian delicatessens where regional specialities are available.

Salt Cod
Known as *baccalà*, this is cod which is preserved by salting and drying. It is used in a variety of dishes. Available from Italian delicatessens but fresh cod can be substituted.

White Truffles
These are from the Piedmont region of Italy. They have a stronger flavour than the black ones but they are not as common. Look in Italian delicatessens but if they are not available then substitute black truffles.

From Apulia: *Fried Sweet Peppers and Tomatoes (page 38)*

Piedmont

Piedmont, in the extreme north of Italy, is a region of extreme contrasts, ranging from the snow-capped peaks of the Alps to the peaceful vineyards, orchards and olive groves. Piedmontese cooking relies heavily on the use of butter and wine, and game and dairy produce are bountiful.

A meal in Piedmont would probably start with a soup, or perhaps a regional version of that well-known pasta speciality, ravioli. For the main course, the central dish could be one of hare, veal or beef in a red wine sauce.

Risotto and courgettes are as common here as they are to Italian cooking in general, so they would be a likely addition to the meal. When it comes to the sweet course, that most famous of Italian desserts – Zabaione – is native to this region. Enriched with the full flavour of Marsala, the sweet Sicilian wine, this dessert is made from eggs and a little sugar. Whipped over hot water until thickened and very foamy, then served with crisp, light fingers of sponge cake, this custard is the perfect complement to a rich main course.

No Italian meal is complete without plenty of wine with which to wash down the various dishes. From this northern area of Italy comes that well-known sparkling wine, Asti Spumante. However, the better choice to accompany food would be a Barolc not only one of the most famous but also one of the best wines from northern Italy.

HOT GARLIC AND ANCHOVY SAUCE

SERVES 6

Raw vegetables, such as carrots, artichoke hearts, fennel stalks, cauliflower and radishes, are dipped into this delicious hot sauce which is one of the gastronomic specialities of Piedmont, and is reputed to date from the early 18th Century.

5 cloves garlic
300 ml/½ pint milk
4 (50-g/2-oz) cans anchovy fillets,
drained
1 head celery
3 tablespoons lemon juice
300 ml/½ pint olive oil
50 g/2 oz butter
6 slices fresh bread

Peel and finely chop the garlic and soak it in half the milk for 2 hours. Soak the anchovy fillets in the remaining milk for 10 to 15 minutes, to remove the excess salt. Trim off the celery roots and leaves, discard any bruised stalks, then wash thoroughly. Cut the stalks into 2.5-cm/1-in pieces. Place in a bowl of cold water and add the lemon juice.

Drain the garlic. Drain the anchovy fillets and pound them to a paste. Heat the olive oil and butter in a small saucepan over a very low heat; add the anchovy paste and mix well. Add the garlic and continue cooking very gently for 20 minutes, stirring occasionally.

Pour the sauce into a chafing dish and place it over a low heat in the middle of the table. Place the bowl of celery pieces on the table beside it. Each diner takes a piece of bread in one hand and a fork in the other. He or she spears a piece of celery on the fork. The celery is then dried on a napkin, dipped in the sauce and eaten. This sauce, known in Italy as *bagna cauda*, is usually accompanied by a young wine such as Barbera.

Note Traditionally, the remaining sauce is used up by breaking several eggs into it and scrambling it.

From Piedmont: *Stewed Beef in Red Wine Sauce (page 17)*

STUFFED PASTA

SERVES 6

In Italy there are various types of stuffed pasta. The names, shapes and fillings vary from region to region. The charmingly descriptive Italian name for these – *agnolotti* – means 'little fat lambs'.

For the filling
2 tablespoons Italian rice (or other
long-grain rice)
100 g/4 oz butter
I small onion, finely chopped
I small carrot, finely chopped
I stick celery, finely chopped
I tablespoon chopped parsley
225 g/8 oz minced beef
150 ml/¼ pint dry white wine
3–4 medium-sized tomatoes, peeled,
deseeded and chopped
4 parboiled cabbage leaves, shredded
pinch of ground nutmeg
salt and pepper
25 g/1 oz Parmesan cheese, grated
2 eggs
For the pasta
6 eggs
I tablespoon olive oil
450 g/1 lb plain flour
I teaspoon salt
I egg, beaten
To serve
½ quantity Meat Sauce (page 64),
heated or 225 g/8 oz melted butter,
flavoured with I teaspoon dried sage
100 g/4 oz Parmesan cheese, grated

To make the filling, cook the rice in lightly-salted, boiling water for about 15 minutes or until *al dente* (cooked but still firm). Drain well and set aside.

Heat half the butter in a saucepan over a moderate heat. Add the onion, carrot, celery and parsley and sauté until lightly browned, stirring frequently. Add the beef, mix well and cook for 3 to 4 minutes. Pour the wine over the beef and boil, uncovered, until the liquid is reduced to I teaspoon. Add the tomatoes, rice, cabbage, remaining butter, nutmeg and salt and pepper to taste. Continue cooking the mixture until it becomes thick. Remove the saucepan from the heat and stir in the cheese and the eggs. Set aside to cool.

To make the pasta, lightly whisk together the eggs and olive oil in a small bowl. Sift the flour and salt on to a marble slab or into a mixing bowl and make a well in the centre. Pour in the eggs and the

oil. Mix to a firm, smooth dough. Knead well. Wrap in a damp cloth and set aside for about 30 minutes.

Roll the dough into two large sheets, about 2 mm/1⁄16 in thick, and brush with the beaten egg. Place the filling in a piping bag, fitted with a large plain nozzle, and pipe out small amounts of filling about 2.5 cm/1 in apart on the first sheet of dough. Cover with the second sheet of dough and press firmly around each mound of filling with the fingertips to seal the layers of dough together and to completely enclose the filling. With a 5-cm/2-in floured cutter, cut out the stuffed pasta. Alternatively, cut them into squares with a floured, sharp knife. Arrange the circles on a lightly-floured surface, making sure that they do not touch, and set aside.

To serve the pasta, cook about 15 minutes in plenty of lightly-salted, boiling water. Drain well and layer in a large, oval, heated serving dish with a little of the hot meat sauce or the flavoured melted butter between the layers. Serve the cheese separately.

POTATO GNOCCHI WITH CHEESE

SERVES 6

Gnocchi may look as doughy and uninteresting as their name implies. *Gnocco* (the singular of *gnocchi*) is a dialect word for 'dullard' or 'puddinghead'.

1.75 kg/4 lb potatoes
salt
2 egg yolks
350 g/12 oz plain flour
100 g/4 oz butter
I quantity Tomato Sauce (page 36)
175 g/6 oz Fontina or Gruyère cheese,
finely sliced
100 g/4 oz Parmesan cheese, grated

Scrub the potatoes under cold running water. Place them in a saucepan and cover with lightly-salted, cold water. Place the saucepan over a moderate heat and bring to the boil; lower the heat and simmer until barely tender. Drain and peel the potatoes, then press them through a sieve on to a marble slab or into a mixing bowl. While still warm, make a well in the centre and add the egg yolks and three-quarters of the flour. Mix to a soft

From Lombardy: *Broth with Poached Eggs*
(page 20)

STEWED BEEF IN RED WINE SAUCE

SERVES 6

(Illustrated on page 15)

Some of the best wines are produced in Piedmont where Barola has been famous for centuries. Barbaresco is a similar but somewhat less alcoholic Piedmontese wine.

1.25 kg/2½ lb beef topside
2 rashers lean bacon, cut into matchstick strips
1 small carrot, cut into matchstick strips
1 medium-sized onion, chopped
1 stick celery, chopped
generous 450 ml/¾ pint Barola or dry red wine
2 cloves garlic
4 dried mushrooms, soaked for 20 minutes and drained, or 4 fresh mushrooms
100 g/4 oz ham fat
4 peppercorns
small bay leaf
flour for coating
salt and pepper
3 tablespoons brandy

dough, adding a little more flour, if necessary. Knead lightly until smooth.

Divide the dough and, with floured hands, form it into long rolls about 2.5 cm/1 in. in diameter. Cut the rolls into 3.5-cm/1½-in pieces and make a lengthways groove on either side of each piece by pressing between the index and second fingers. Arrange them on a lightly-floured surface, making sure that they do not touch. Set aside for 10 to 15 minutes to dry.

Place a few *gnocchi* at a time into a large saucepan half-filled with lightly-salted, boiling water. As they come to the surface, remove them with a perforated spoon. Drain them well and place them on a large heated plate to keep hot. Heat the butter in a heavy saucepan until lightly browned. Heat the tomato sauce.

Cover the *gnocchi* with the cheese slices and sprinkle with the browned butter. Serve immediately, accompanied by the tomato sauce and Parmesan cheese.

Using a sharp knife, make incisions all over the beef and insert the bacon and carrot strips. Place the beef in a shallow bowl with half the onion, celery and wine. Set aside to marinate for eight hours, turning the meat occasionally.

Peel and crush the garlic, chop the mushrooms and heat the ham fat in a large saucepan over a low heat. Add the remaining onion, garlic, peppercorns and bay leaf and sauté until golden-brown, stirring occasionally. Remove the beef from the marinade, dry well and coat with the flour. Reserve the marinade. Brown the beef on all sides in the saucepan. Lower the heat and add the mushrooms and marinade. Season with salt and pepper and simmer over a moderate heat for about 3 hours, or until tender, adding a little water occasionally as the sauce thickens.

Remove the beef from the saucepan, slice it and place on a warmed serving dish. Strain the sauce through a fine sieve into a small saucepan and place it over a low heat. Heat the brandy gently in a second small saucepan. When it is reduced to 2 tablespoons, ignite and quickly stir it into the sauce. Pour the hot sauce over the meat and serve immediately.

PIEDMONT BRAISED BEEF

SERVES 6

Polenta is the national dish of Italy. Today it is made with corn meal but the ancient Romans used millet or spelt, a primitive type of wheat. Then known as *pulmentum*, it served as field rations for the Roman soldiers.

1.25 kg/2½ lb chuck or blade steak
pinch of salt and pepper
lard or oil for frying
5 medium-sized onions, sliced
600 ml/1 pint dry red wine
¼ quantity Meat Sauce (page 64)
1 quantity Polenta (page 25)

Cut the beef into slices about 1 cm/½ in thick; flatten them lightly with a meat mallet or a rolling pin. Sprinkle with salt and pepper. Heat the lard or oil in a frying pan over a moderate heat and sauté the beef on each side until lightly browned. Remove the meat from the frying pan and drain it on kitchen paper, reserving the fat in the pan.

Meanwhile, put the onions in a saucepan and cover them with water. Simmer them for 5 minutes. Remove the onions with a perforated spoon and drain well on kitchen paper. Sauté the onions in the lard remaining in the frying pan until lightly browned. Add a pinch of salt.

Lightly grease a 2-litre/3½-pint pie dish and fill it with half the onions. Place the beef on top and cover with the remaining onions. Add the wine and the meat sauce. Place in a cool oven (150C, 300F, gas 2) and cook for 2½ hours, or until the beef is tender and the liquid has evaporated. Serve very hot with the *Polenta*.

HARE IN RED WINE SAUCE

SERVES 6

1 (1.5-kg/3-lb) hare, chopped into portions
½ small onion, sliced
¼ stick celery, chopped
1 clove garlic, peeled and crushed
2 peppercorns
pinch of dried thyme
small bay leaf
pinch of salt
600 ml/1 pint dry red wine
For the sauce
50 g/2 oz butter
1 medium-sized onion, sliced
1 small carrot, sliced
salt
2 teaspoons plain flour
225 g/8 oz fresh button mushrooms, quartered
1 tablespoon dry red wine
5 tablespoons brandy
1 quantity Polenta (page 25)

Wipe the hare portions with a damp cloth and place in a large dish. Add the onion, celery and garlic to the hare with the peppercorns, thyme, bay leaf and salt. Pour the wine over and set aside to marinate for 4 to 5 hours, turning occasionally. Remove the hare from the marinade and dry well with kitchen paper. Reserve the marinade.

To make the sauce, melt two-thirds of the butter in a heavy-based saucepan over a moderate heat, add the onion and carrot and sauté until lightly browned. Add the hare and sauté until brown. Add salt to taste and sprinkle in the flour, stirring constantly. When the flour begins to brown, add the marinade. Bring the liquid slowly to the boil, still stirring. Lower the heat, cover the pan tightly, and simmer the hare for 1¼ hours.

Place the remaining butter in a large saucepan; add the mushrooms and sauté for 2 to 3 minutes. Remove the hare from the sauce and add to the mushrooms. Strain the sauce through a fine sieve and pour it over the hare. Reheat and adjust the seasoning.

Meanwhile, heat the brandy gently in a small saucepan. Ignite, and while it is still flaming, quickly pour it over the hare. Place the hare and sauce in a heated serving dish. Serve hot with slices of *Polenta* lightly fried in oil.

WHITE SAUCE
MAKES ABOUT 450 ml/¾ pint

This is a basic white sauce. Nutmeg is much used by Italians in milk and cheese dishes.

75 g/3 oz butter
2 teaspoons finely chopped onion
50 g/2 oz plain flour, sifted
450 ml/¾ pint milk
pinch of ground nutmeg
salt and pepper

Heat the butter in a saucepan over a moderate heat. Add the onion and sauté until it is soft but not brown. Sprinkle the flour over the butter and stir for 1 to 2 minutes over a low heat. Add the milk gradually, mixing thoroughly after each addition. Add the nutmeg, salt and pepper. Bring the sauce to the boil, stirring constantly until it thickens. Continue cooking over a very low heat for 15 minutes.

From Lombardy: *Minestrone (page 21)*

ZABAIONE
SERVES 6

This is one of the most famous of Italian desserts. Quickly prepared, it is an ideal 'emergency' dish and despite tasting very rich, it is surprisingly low in calories.

3 egg yolks
75 g/3 oz caster sugar
2 teaspoons cold water
5 tablespoons sweet white wine or
Marsala

Put the egg yolks, sugar and cold water in the top half of a double boiler or in a large ovenproof bowl over hot water. Stir until the mixture is smooth and slightly thickened, then gradually pour in the wine. Whisk vigorously until thick and foamy. Remove the double boiler from the heat and stir the mixture until slightly cooled. Pour into individual glass bowls and serve immediately.

Lombardy

Stretching from the Alps southwards to the River Po, Lombardy is a region which boasts a cosmopolitan style of cooking. The successive occupations by Romans, Huns and Goths, Hungarians and Spaniards have contributed this characteristic. In Milan, butter is used extensively in cooking and polenta (the Italian corn meal pudding), is almost as popular here as it is in Venice.

Lombardy produces excellent veal, and the Milanese claim to make the very best Minestrone in Italy. Another classic dish of the region is the Risotto alla Milanese in which basic rice is enriched with white wine and, traditionally, bone marrow.

As in other areas of Italy, food is considered to be a most important part of the culture and it is quite common for small towns to treasure their own favourite recipes for local specialities. As well as the many flavoursome savoury dishes, sweet delights like torrone (a type of nougat) are also found here.

The region produces an immense variety of cheeses, of which Gorgonzola and Bel Paese are the best known. Prodigious amounts of crespone or salame Milano are produced and what cannot be eaten is exported to give Britain the most popular Italian salami.

Lombardy has no great wines but a number of pleasing ones. Some very palatable wines are produced and Campari is made in this region.

BROTH WITH POACHED EGGS

SERVES I

(Illustrated on page 17)

Francis I, King of France, losing the battle of Pavia and pursued by the Spaniards, stopped at a cottage and asked for food. The cook was preparing minestrone, and, endeavouring to enrich this classic vegetable soup to befit the illustrious visitor, she toasted and buttered slices of bread, topped them with eggs and Parmesan cheese and poured the boiling soup over the top. Today a simple chicken broth is usually served, instead of minestrone.

300 ml/½ pint good chicken stock
1–2 eggs
salt and pepper
1 slice bread
50 g/2 oz butter
40 g/1½ oz Parmesan cheese, grated

Pour the stock into an ovenproof dish and carefully add the eggs, without breaking the yolks. Season with salt and pepper. Place the dish in a preheated, moderately hot oven (190C, 375F, gas 5) for 5 to 10 minutes or just long enough to lightly set the eggs.

Meanwhile, spread the slice of bread with some of the butter; sprinkle it with a little of the cheese, and cut it into quarters. Sauté the bread in the remaining butter until golden brown. Arrange the pieces of fried bread in the soup, surrounding the eggs, and bring to the table. Serve with the remaining Parmesan cheese.

Note Some Italians break the egg into a bowl and pour the boiling broth over the eggs; however, this does not sufficiently cook the eggs for some tastes.

MINESTRONE

SERVES 6

(Illustrated on page 19)

*50 g/2 oz dried borlotti or haricot
beans
100 g/4 oz rindless lean, mild-cured
bacon in 1 piece
100 g/4 oz butter
½ small onion, chopped
1 leek, coarsely chopped
bouquet garni
225 g/8 oz tomatoes, peeled
salt and freshly milled black pepper
1 medium-sized potato, diced
1 large carrot, scraped and diced
1 medium-sized aubergine, peeled
and diced
350 g/12 oz fresh peas, shelled
1 small celery heart, sliced
2 litres/3½ pints chicken stock
225 g/8 oz Italian rice (or other long-
grain rice)
1 clove garlic
100 g/4 oz Parmesan cheese, grated*

From Lombardy: *Beef-stuffed Pasta with Herb Butter (page 23)*

Soak the beans in cold water for 24 hours. Drain well and cook in lightly salted boiling water for about 1 hour, or until tender. Drain before using. Simmer the bacon in boiling water for 15 to 20 minutes. Drain well and cut into 5-mm/¼-in cubes.

Heat one-third of the butter in a saucepan over a moderate heat and add the bacon, onion, leek and the bouquet garni. Cook for 3 to 4 minutes. Remove the bouquet garni, then add the tomatoes and season to taste. Simmer gently.

Heat the remaining butter in a second saucepan and sauté the potatoes, carrot, aubergine, peas and celery over a moderate heat for 5 to 8 minutes. Add to the tomato mixture, simmer for 2 to 3 minutes, then pour in the stock. Simmer over a moderate heat until the vegetables are tender. Increase the heat and when the stock boils, add the rice and simmer until *al dente* (cooked but still firm). Peel and chop the garlic. A few moments before serving, add the garlic. Serve with the cheese.

Note In summer, this soup may be served chilled. As soon as the rice is cooked *al dente*, season immediately with the garlic, then pour the soup into soup plates. Chill until required.

SPINACH-STUFFED PASTA

SERVES 6

For the pasta
5 eggs
1 tablespoon olive oil
450 g/1 lb plain flour
1 teaspoon salt
For the filling
275 g/10 oz dried breadcrumbs
175 g/6 oz Parmesan cheese, grated
1 (227-g/8 oz) packet frozen chopped spinach, thawed and drained
salt and pepper
pinch of ground nutmeg
2 egg yolks
1–2 tablespoons beef stock (optional)
1 beaten egg
175 g/6 oz butter, melted
100 g/4 oz Parmesan cheese, grated

Lightly whisk the eggs and olive oil together in a small bowl. Sift the flour and salt onto a marble slab or into a mixing bowl and make a well in the centre. Pour in the eggs and oil, mix to a firm smooth

From Lombardy: *Spinach-stuffed Pasta*

dough and knead well. Wrap in a damp cloth and set aside for about 30 minutes.

To make the filling, mix together the breadcrumbs, cheese, spinach, salt, pepper and nutmeg. Add the egg yolks and mix to a soft dough, adding the stock to moisten if necessary.

Roll the dough into two thin sheets, about 2 mm/$\frac{1}{16}$in thick. Brush the surface of the first sheet of pasta with beaten egg and, using a piping bag fitted with 1-cm/$\frac{1}{2}$-in nozzle, pipe small amounts of filling on to the sheet about 5 cm/2 in apart. Cover with a second sheet of pasta, brush with the egg and seal the layers together by pressing the spaces between the filling with the fingertips.

Cut into squares, using a pastry wheel or a sharp knife, and arrange on a lightly floured board. Cook the pasta, a few pieces at a time, in a large saucepan half-filled with lightly salted boiling water for 8 to 10 minutes, or until they rise to the surface. Remove with a perforated spoon and drain well.

Meanwhile, heat the butter in a saucepan over a moderate heat until it is lightly browned. Arrange the pasta in layers in a heated serving dish sprinkled with the butter and half the cheese. Serve immediately with the remaining cheese.

BEEF-STUFFED PASTA WITH HERB BUTTER

SERVES 6

(Illustrated on page 21)

In Lombardy, these stuffed pasta squares are traditionally served with herb butter made with sage and grated Parmesan cheese. Some very old recipes indicate that the stuffing was composed of pears, almonds and chopped, mixed candied peel.

For the pasta
5 eggs
I tablespoon butter, melted
450 g/1 lb plain flour
I teaspoon salt
For the filling
25 g/1 oz butter
2 cloves garlic, peeled and finely chopped
I tablespoon chopped parsley
225 g/8 oz minced beef
2 tablespoons fine fresh breadcrumbs
I tablespoon grated Parmesan cheese
pinch of ground nutmeg
salt and pepper
I–2 eggs
To serve
175 g/6 oz butter
crushed sage leaves
100 g/4 oz Parmesan cheese, grated

To make the pasta, lightly whisk the eggs and butter in a small bowl. Sift the flour and salt on to a marble slab or into a mixing bowl and make a well in the centre. Pour in the egg mixture, mix to a firm dough and knead well. Wrap in a damp cloth and set aside for about 30 minutes.

To make the filling, heat the butter in a frying pan over a moderate heat. Add the garlic and parsley and sauté until they begin to brown. Add the beef and sauté for about 10 minutes, stirring frequently. Remove the frying pan from the heat, add the breadcrumbs and cheese and set aside in a bowl to cool. Season with the nutmeg and salt and pepper to taste and blend to a paste with the eggs.

Roll the dough into sheets, about 2 mm/$\frac{1}{16}$ in thick, on a lightly floured surface. Cut the dough into 10-cm/4-in squares and put I tablespoon of the filling on half of each square. Brush the edges of the square with water, fold the uncovered half of the square over the filling and press the edges together to completely enclose the filling. Place on a lightly floured tray until required, then lower a few at a time into a large saucepan half filled with lightly salted boiling water. Cook for about 5 minutes, removing them with a perforated spoon as they rise to the surface. Drain well and place on a heated serving dish.

To serve, heat the butter until golden brown, sprinkle it with crushed sage leaves to taste and pour this sauce over the pasta. Sprinkle with the cheese and serve immediately.

MILANESE-STYLE VEAL CUTLETS

SERVES 6

In days gone by, the servants rose at dawn to beat the cutlets rhythmically on wood, first one side, then the other. It was thought that only this treatment would make the meat tender.

6 veal neck cutlets
pepper
100 g/4 oz plain flour
2 eggs, beaten
100 g/4 oz browned breadcrumbs
100 g/4 oz butter
salt
3 lemons, quartered lengthways
pinch of ground nutmeg (optional)

Remove the T-shaped bone from the top of each cutlet, leaving the meat attached to the long rib bone. Remove and discard any skin and excess fat, and flatten the veal with a meat mallet or a rolling pin. Season the veal with pepper and dip the slices in the flour. Then dip them in the eggs and the breadcrumbs.

About 15 to 20 minutes before serving, heat the butter in a frying pan over a moderate heat and sauté the veal for 10 to 15 minutes, or until the slices are lightly browned on each side.

Arrange the cutlets on a heated serving dish and sprinkle them with the butter in which they were cooked. Sprinkle with salt. Garnish with the lemons and serve immediately. A pinch of nutmeg may be sprinkled over the cutlets.

MILANESE RISOTTO WITH WHITE WINE

SERVES 6

Many Milanese dishes, including this *risotto*, are coloured with saffron, derived from the belief in 14th Century Milan that if food was served gilded, it would cure illness.

225 g/8 oz butter
1 tablespoon chopped onion
pinch of pepper
150 ml/¼ pint dry white wine
450 g/1 lb Italian rice (or other long-grain rice)
salt
pinch of powdered saffron
about 1 litre/1¾ pints vegetable stock
100 g/4 oz Parmesan cheese, grated
parsley sprigs to garnish

Melt one-third of the butter in a saucepan over a low heat and add the onion and pepper. Sauté the onion until soft, but not browned, then add the wine and reduce the liquid by half. Add the rice and salt and cook for 2 to 3 minutes, stirring constantly. Add the powdered saffron and stock and bring to the boil, still stirring. Simmer for about 15 minutes, stirring constantly and adding a little additional hot stock, if necessary, to prevent the rice from sticking to the saucepan.

Remove the saucepan from the heat when the rice is *al dente* (cooked but still firm). Add the remaining butter and 2 to 3 tablespoons of the cheese. Set aside for 2 to 3 minutes in a warm place, then transfer to a heated serving dish. Serve immediately with the remaining cheese. Garnish with a sprig of parsley.

TURKEY WITH CHESTNUT STUFFING

SERVES 6

In this recipe the turkey is boned and then stuffed, although some Lombard cooks prefer to leave the turkey whole and stuff the cavity with the mixture. The roasting time is reduced slightly in this case. Italian dried chestnuts may be used instead of fresh ones, in which case only 225 g/8 oz will be needed. Dried chestnuts should be soaked overnight and are then ready for use.

1 (3.5–4.5 kg/8–10 lb) turkey
450 g/1 lb chestnuts
100 g/4 oz very lean rindless bacon
225 g/8 oz prunes, soaked, stoned and chopped
1 medium-sized cooking apple, peeled, cored and sliced
2 medium-sized pears, peeled, cored and sliced
1 small white truffle, sliced (optional)
225 g/8 oz sausagemeat
salt and pepper
3 tablespoons brandy
1 very thin slice rindless bacon fat
25 g/1 oz butter, melted
300 ml/½ pint vegetable stock
2 tablespoons lemon juice
15 g/½ oz butter

To prepare the turkey, break off the wings and the legs at the first joints. Using a very sharp knife, open the turkey along the back-bone from the neck to tail. Ease out the bones from inside the wings, little by little. Working from the inside, remove the bones from the legs. Remove all the remaining bones from the carcass.

Split the chestnut skins with a sharp knife and roast them in a preheated, moderately hot oven (200 C, 400 F, gas 6) for 40 to 50 minutes. Remove the chestnuts from the oven and set them aside to cool. Remove and discard the outer and inner skins and coarsely chop the nuts. Simmer the bacon for 5 minutes in boiling water, drain and cut into fine strips.

Place the chestnuts, prunes, bacon, apple, pears, and truffle in a large mixing bowl with the sausagemeat. Season with salt and pepper and the brandy and mix thoroughly. Stuff the turkey with the mixture and sew it up securely along the back-

bone. Sprinkle with salt and pepper and cover the breast with the slices of bacon fat. Truss the turkey into its original shape with fine white string.

Place the turkey in a buttered roasting tin and roast in a preheated, moderately hot oven (200 C, 400 F, gas 6) for 20 minutes. Reduce the heat to moderate (160 C, 325 F, gas 3) and roast for a further 2 hours.

About 20 minutes before the end of the cooking time, remove the turkey from the oven and discard the slices of fat. Brush the turkey with the melted butter and return it to the oven. During the last 10 minutes, season with salt and pepper.

Remove the turkey from the roasting tin and place it on a heated serving dish. Remove and discard the string. Let the turkey stand at room temperature for 15 to 20 minutes to make it easier to carve. Meanwhile, mix the stock into the juices left in the pan, simmer for 2 to 3 minutes, stirring with a wooden spoon to prevent the gravy from sticking. Strain through a fine sieve, skim off the fat and stir in the lemon juice and the butter. Serve the gravy separately.

From Lombardy: _Milanese Risotto with White Wine (opposite)_

POLENTA
SERVES 6

1 litre/ 1¾ pints water
1 teaspoon salt
350 g/ 12 oz yellow corn meal

Bring the water and salt to the boil in a large heavy saucepan. Sprinkle in one-third of the corn meal, a little at a time, stirring constantly. As the mixture thickens, add 2 to 3 tablespoons boiling water. After 15 minutes, sprinkle in another third of the corn meal, stirring constantly, then add the remaining corn meal and stir until well blended.

The polenta is cooked in about 30 to 40 minutes when it comes away easily from the side of the pan. To make the corn meal easier to digest, and to remove its slightly bitter taste, cook for 1 hour. Serve hot with various sauces and garnishes, or cold cut into slices, with butter and freshly grated Parmesan cheese. It may also be cut into thick slices and fried. Sliced cold polenta is a good substitute for bread, especially with a beef stew.

Veneto

Sugar and spice were introduced to Europe by the Venetian traders who founded their vast fortunes on imports from the Orient. So, to this day, Venetian food is characteristically sweet and spicy. And the bright colours of the east make the Venice food markets one of Italy's most colourful spectacles.

For hundreds of years, food has been a Venetian obsession. There are many contemporary paintings of sumptuous Venetian banquets at which exotic foods were washed down with fine wines from exquisite glassware.

Corn was another Venetian introduction and it is used to make polenta which is eaten with almost everything! This can be boiled, fried or baked to be eaten instead of bread, with butter and cheese. Although polenta and rice are widely used, this is not to the exclusion of pasta dishes which are also served in various forms. Spices and herbs, such as nutmeg, saffron and mint are used fairly heavily in dishes from this region.

Fish and shellfish are available in profusion and are used in all sorts of hot dishes and seafood salads. Many of these local delicacies are unknown elsewhere.

Lastly, the wines of this region offer two familiar options. The best white Italian wines, Soave, is from this area and that much loved red wine, Valpolicella, is also local to Veneto.

BEEF BROTH WITH DUMPLINGS

SERVES 6

This is a delicious light soup. The tiny dumplings are cooked in plain boiling water before being strained and added to the broth, so as not to cloud the pleasing clearness of the broth.

2 eggs
450 ml/$\frac{3}{4}$ pint milk
100 g/4 oz butter
$\frac{1}{2}$ onion, chopped
1 tablespoon chopped parsley
100 g/4 oz finely chopped, smoked bacon fat
450 g/1 lb stale white bread, crusts removed, cubed
75 g/3 oz plain flour
salt
2 litres/3$\frac{1}{2}$ pints beef broth

Whisk the eggs and milk together. Heat the butter in a frying pan over a moderate heat, add the onion and parsley and sauté until lightly browned. Add the bacon fat and heat gently for 2 to 3 minutes. Add the bread and sauté until lightly browned.

Remove the frying pan from the heat, transfer the contents to a bowl and set aside to cool. Add the flour and the egg mixture and blend to form a firm paste. Set aside for 15 minutes. Wet your hands and shape the paste into balls about the size of a walnut. Drop into lightly salted, boiling water and simmer for about 4 to 5 minutes, or until they rise to the surface. Remove the dumplings with a perforated spoon and drain well.

Bring the broth to the boil and add the cooked, well drained, dumplings. Simmer for 2 to 3 minutes in the broth, then serve immediately.

CHILLED SOLE WITH SULTANAS IN WINE SAUCE

SERVES 6

This dish is served on the night of the Feast of the Holy Redeemer, on the 3rd Sunday in July. There are great celebrations, culminating in a firework display.

> *3 (350-g/12-oz) sole, filleted*
> *salt and pepper*
> *about 100 g/4 oz plain flour*
> *150 ml/¼ pint olive oil*
> *1 medium-sized onion, thinly sliced*
> *2 small carrots, thinly sliced*
> *1 small celery heart, thinly sliced*
> *2 bay leaves*
> *25 g/1 oz sultanas*
> *25 g/1 oz pine kernels*
> *300 ml/½ pint dry white wine*
> *300 ml/½ pint vinegar*

Use a meat mallet or a wooden rolling pin dipped in cold water to very gently flatten the fillets. Dry

From Veneto: *Creamed Salt Cod (overleaf)*

them with a cloth or kitchen paper. Season the fillets with salt and pepper and dip them in the flour.

Heat about half the olive oil in a frying pan over a moderate heat. Add the fillets and sauté them for about 3 to 4 minutes on each side. Drain well and place them on a serving dish. Pour the remaining olive oil into the frying pan, add the onion, carrots, celery, bay leaves and a little salt. Sauté over a high heat, then arrange the mixture over the fish. Sprinkle with the sultanas and pine kernels. Pour the wine and vinegar into the frying pan and boil to reduce the liquid by half. Pour this over the fish, set aside to cool. Chill before serving.

BAKED SEA BASS

SERVES 6

(Illustrated on page 30)

Bass is found in temperate waters and used to be a popular fish in the days of Ancient Rome. It is particularly good baked in the oven, as in this recipe.

1 (1.5-kg/3-lb) sea bass
salt and pepper
50 g/2 oz butter
1 tablespoon olive oil
1 medium-sized onion, sliced
Garnish
1 head endive, washed
2 lemons, quartered lengthways

Make a diagonal slit on each side of the fish to help the heat to penetrate while cooking. Season it with salt and pepper. Place the fish in a casserole with the butter and olive oil. Arrange the onion slices over the fish. Bake in a preheated moderately hot oven (190C, 375F, gas 5) for 45 to 50 minutes, or until the flesh of the fish is firm and white. Baste occasionally with the cooking juices.

Carefully remove the fish from the casserole and place it on a heated serving dish. Arrange the endive and lemons around the fish. Strain the juices left in the casserole, pour them over the fish and serve.

CREAMED SALT COD

SERVES 6

(Illustrated on previous page)

This fish dish is frequently served as the Friday 'fast day' meal throughout Italy and in this area in particular. Dried salt cod is also known as stock-fish. It can be bought in Indian grocers.

575 g/ 1¼ lb dried salt cod
3 cloves garlic, peeled
600–900 ml/ 1-1½ pints milk
3 tablespoons olive oil
pinch of ground cinnamon
salt and pepper
1 quantity Polenta (page 25)

Soak the fish for 2 days in plenty of cold water, changing the water frequently. Drain it, rinse it under cold running water and dry it. Remove and discard any skin and bones and thinly slice the fish. Rub the garlic around the inside of a flameproof casserole or a large saucepan.

Place the fish in the casserole and add enough milk to cover it. Place the casserole over a moderate heat and simmer until the mixture begins to darken in colour. While the fish cooks, break it into small pieces with a wooden spoon. Heat the remaining milk and gradually stir it into the casserole together with the olive oil to obtain a soft purée. It may not be necessary to add all of the milk. Season with the cinnamon and salt and pepper to taste. Serve hot with warm slices of *Polenta*.

Note If you cannot obtain dried salt cod, then use 1 kg/2 lb fresh cod. Skin the fish and cook in just enough milk to cover; less milk will be required to produce a soft purée.

SQUID AND HARICOT BEAN SALAD

SERVES 6

450 g/ 1 lb haricot beans
1 large onion
1 large carrot
1 stick celery
1 litre/ 1¾ pints water
salt and pepper
450 g/ 1 lb prepared squid, thickly sliced
4 tablespoons olive oil
3 tablespoons lemon juice
6 hard-boiled eggs

Soak the beans overnight in cold water. Drain and cook in plenty of lightly salted boiling water for about 45 to 50 minutes, or until tender. Drain and set aside.

Put the onion, carrot and celery in a large saucepan with the water, salt and pepper. Bring to the boil, then simmer for 5 minutes. Add the squid and simmer for about 1 hour, or until tender. Drain and set aside to cool. Discard the vegetables but reserve 2–3 tablespoons of the stock for the dressing.

Mix the olive oil, lemon juice, stock and seasoning to taste. Slice the hard-boiled eggs. Place the beans and squid in a salad bowl and pour over the dressing. Garnish with the eggs. Mix together at the table before serving.

RICE AND SHELLFISH SALAD

SERVES 6

In Italy, rice is often served as a salad. It is the addition of saffron, together with the shellfish, which gives this recipe a typically Venetian flavour.

600 ml/1 pint clams
600 ml/1 pint mussels
600 ml/1 pint cockles
3 tablespoons dry white wine
100 g/4 oz uncooked scampi (optional)
450 g/1 lb Italian rice (or other long-grain rice)
3 hard-boiled eggs
3 tablespoons olive oil
pinch of saffron powder
few drops Worcestershire sauce
salt and pepper
1 tablespoon chopped parsley

Scrape the clams, mussels and cockles and rinse them well under cold running water. Discard any open shellfish. Place them in a large saucepan with the wine, cover tightly and place over a high heat.

From Veneto: *Rice and Shellfish Salad*

Shake the saucepan gently until the shells open. Drain.

Remove the fish from the shells, discard the shells and any unopened shellfish. Peel the scampi (if used) and simmer in lightly salted, boiling water for 4 to 5 minutes. Drain well and dice them. Cook the rice in plenty of lightly salted boiling water for 15 to 20 minutes or until *al dente* (cooked but still firm). Drain and set aside to cool.

Pound the eggs to a paste, using a pestle and mortar, or a liquidiser. Add the oil gradually, beating constantly. Add the saffron powder and Worcestershire sauce. Season with salt and pepper to taste.

Mix the rice with the fish. Place in a glass dish and cover with the sauce. Sprinkle with the parsley. Toss the salad at the table just before serving.

Note If clams are not available, increase the quantities of mussels and cockles accordingly.

CHICKEN RISOTTO

SERVES 6

This dish was said to be so popular with the Austrian police during their occupation, that it became known as 'policemen's *risotto*'.

900-g/2-lb chicken or chicken joints
1 small carrot
1 small onion
2 sticks celery, chopped
350 g/12 oz tomatoes, peeled
225 g/8 oz boneless lean stewing veal
salt and pepper
100 g/4 oz butter
100 g/4 oz finely chopped smoked bacon fat
1 tablespoon chopped onion
1 tablespoon chopped carrot
150 ml/¼ pint dry white wine
450 g/1 lb Italian rice (or other long-grain rice)
100 g/4 oz Parmesan cheese, grated

Bone the chicken and reserve the bones and any giblets. Cut the flesh into 1-cm/½-in cubes. Place the chicken bones, giblets and veal in a saucepan

From Veneto: *Baked Sea Bass (page 28)*

with the carrot, onion, celery stick and a pinch of salt. Cover with water and place over a moderate heat and bring to the boil. Lower the heat and simmer gently for 30 to 40 minutes. Strain through a sieve and discard the chicken bones and the vegetables. The veal may be reserved and used in another dish.

Heat 25 g/1 oz of the butter in a saucepan. Add the bacon fat, chopped celery, onion and carrot and sauté until lightly browned. Add the chicken, season with salt and pepper to taste, cover tightly and cook for 3 to 4 minutes. Add the wine and reduce to 1 tablespoon. Add the tomatoes and simmer for 8 minutes. Add the rice and three-quarters of the chicken stock. Simmer for about 20 minutes or until the rice is *al dente* (cooked but still firm), adding a little of the remaining stock as the rice absorbs the liquid.

Remove the saucepan from the heat, stir in the remaining butter and 25 g/1 oz of the cheese. Let it stand for 1 to 2 minutes, then turn onto a warmed serving plate. Serve with the remaining cheese.

BRAISED DUCK WITH TURNIPS

SERVES 4

Poulty and game are very popular in Italy. Throughout the ages, cooks have devised unusual ways of preparing duck, turkey, chicken and goose.

1 small onion, sliced
few sprigs thyme
1 bay leaf
few sprigs rosemary
300 ml/½ pint dry red wine
salt and pepper
1 (2-kg/4-lb) duck, cut into 4 pieces
1 tablespoon olive oil
75 g/3 oz butter
25 g/1 oz plain flour
450 ml/¾ pint water
5 tablespoons Tomato Sauce (page 36)
450 g/1 lb turnips, thickly sliced
1 tablespoon chopped onion

To make the marinade, place the onion in a shallow bowl and add the herbs, wine and salt and pepper. Place the duck in the marinade and marinate for 48 hours, stirring occasionally.

Remove the duck from the marinade, drain well and season with salt and pepper. Heat the olive oil and half the butter in a saucepan over a high heat. Add the duck and sauté until well browned. Add the marinade and reduce the liquid by half over high heat. Blend half the flour with a little of the water, then stir it into the marinade. Lower the heat and simmer for 2 to 3 minutes, stirring constantly. Add the remaining water and the tomato sauce. Simmer over a low heat for about 30 minutes, stirring frequently.

Meanwhile, cook the turnips in lightly salted boiling water for 3 minutes. Drain the turnips and reserve the water. Heat the rest of the butter in a frying pan and add the chopped onion. Sauté until lightly browned. Add the remaining flour with about 6 tablespoons of the turnip cooking water and mix thoroughly. Add the turnips and simmer for about 30 minutes.

Remove the duck from the saucepan, drain and place it in a bowl. Strain the sauce through a fine sieve. Replace the duck and the sauce in the saucepan and simmer together for 2 to 3 minutes over a moderate heat. Place the duck in a heated serving dish and pour the sauce over. Serve immediately with the turnips.

BRAISED BEEF WITH POLENTA

SERVES 6

(Illustrated on page 33)

During the 16th Century, a vessel arrived in Venice bearing goods collected on its travels. Among these was a sack of maize. A commonplace sight in America, it caused a sensation in the market of Venice and thereafter *polenta* was made using corn meal. If fresh, grated horseradish is not available, use 4 tablespoons horseradish sauce.

1 kg/2 lb beef topside
salt and pepper
100 g/4 oz bacon fat, cut into matchstick strips
2 tablespoons olive oil
1 small onion, chopped
1 small carrot, chopped
1 stick celery, chopped
1 tablespoon chopped parsley
100 g/4 oz ham fat, chopped
1 clove
freshly ground black pepper
2 tablespoons grated horseradish root
pinch of oregano
about 4 tablespoons vegetable stock or hot water
450 ml/¾ pint tomato juice
1 quantity Polenta (page 25)

Make incisions all over the beef, sprinkle it with salt and pepper, and press the bacon fat strips into the incisions in the beef. Heat the olive oil in a flameproof casserole, add the onion, carrot, celery, parsley and ham fat and sauté until lightly browned. Add the beef and sauté on each side over a high heat until browned. Add the clove, peppercorns, horseradish and oregano.

Remove from the heat, cover with a lid, and place in a preheated moderate oven (180C, 350F, gas 4). Braise for 1 to 1¼ hours, adding 1 tablespoon of stock occasionally to prevent the vegetables from sticking.

Remove the casserole from the oven, mix in the tomato juice, place over a moderate heat and simmer until the juice has reduced to a thick sauce. Remove the beef and carve into slices. Arrange the slices to overlap on an oval, heated serving dish. Strain the sauce and pour it over the beef. Serve immediately with hot *Polenta*.

Campania

Italian cooking is often thought to consist of spaghetti, pizza, olive oil, garlic, tomatoes and cheese and if there is any one region to which this stereotype could be applied, then here it is.

Campania is a region of southern Italy, dominated by Naples where pizza shops proliferate and where the classic pizza napoletana is freshly baked for each hungry customer. Made with the local mozzarella cheese, anchovies and the inevitable olive oil, these pizzas are quite delicious.

Spaghetti and fettucine (ribbon noodles) are served with plenty of olive oil, tomato sauce, cheese and garlic in a variety of dishes. Steak is served with a pizzaiola sauce made from tomatoes and peppers.

Salami from this region is coarse in texture and full flavoured with plenty of seasonings. Its ingredients include pork, beef and significant quantities of pepper.

Rice is not as common here as in some other parts, but tomatoes are put to better use than anywhere else. Surprisingly, there are not as many distinctive fish dishes as in other regions. Naples is famous for its ice cream which is often said to be the best in the world. The wines of this region are not the outstanding ones from Italy. Among them are Lacrima Christi, a strong red or white from the Vesuvian vineyards and Falerno, an undistinguished table wine.

CHICKEN AND BEEF SOUP

SERVES 6

This is really a meal in itself since it is customary to serve the chicken and meat separately as the main course of the meal.

1 (1-kg/2-lb) chicken
450g/1 lb top rump or topside of beef
1 tablespoon coarse salt
1 onion, stuck with 1 clove
1 small carrot
1 stick celery
1 (675-g/1½-lb) cabbage
675g/1½ lb chicory
675g/1½ lb curly endive
2 cloves garlic, chopped
100g/4oz minced ham fat
100g/4oz salami, skinned, in one piece
100g/4oz uncooked ham, in one piece
100g/4oz very lean rindless bacon, in one piece
100g/4oz bacon rind

Place the chicken in a large saucepan with the beef, cover with water and season with the salt. Place over a moderate heat and bring to the boil. Lower the heat and skim the surface. Add the onion, the carrot and celery to the pan. Simmer for 50 to 60 minutes, or until tender. Remove the chicken and beef, drain them and place them in a second saucepan with a little of the broth. Strain the remaining broth through several layers of muslin.

Remove and discard the coarse outer leaves and centre core from the cabbage. Cut the leaves in half. Cut the chicory and curly endive each into quarters lengthways. Place them in a saucepan, cover with lightly salted water and simmer for 4 to 6 minutes. Drain well, rinse under cold running water and squeeze dry. Place the garlic and ham fat in a large saucepan with the partially cooked cabbage, chicory and endive. Add the salami, ham, bacon and the bacon rind and cover with the strained chicken broth.

Place over a high heat and bring to the boil. Lower the heat and simmer for about 2 hours. Remove the salami, ham, bacon and bacon rind, and slice them; return them to the soup. Simmer for 2 to 3 minutes and serve immediately.

Serve the chicken and beef separately as a main course, with vegetables, seasoned with olive oil and garlic.

MACARONI WITH TOMATO, HAM AND CHEESE

SERVES 6

(Illustrated on page 35)

Macaroni is served in numerous ways, this recipe being a very typical one.

575 g/ 1¼ lb macaroni
40 g/ 1½ oz butter
40 g/ 1½ oz lard
3 cloves garlic, peeled and crushed
100 g/4 oz cooked ham, minced
1 kg/2¼ lb tomatoes, peeled and sliced
salt and freshly milled black pepper
1–2 tablespoons coarsely chopped fresh basil
100 g/4 oz Pecorino cheese, grated

Break the macaroni into short pieces and cook it in plenty of lightly salted, boiling water until it is _al dente_ (cooked but still firm). Drain it and reserve it in a warm place.

To make the sauce, heat the butter and lard in a large frying pan or saucepan over a moderate heat. Add the garlic and ham and sauté for 4 to 5 minutes. Add the tomatoes and salt and pepper to taste. Simmer the sauce for 10 to 15 minutes, or until well blended, stirring frequently.

Add the sauce to the macaroni, mix well, and pour into a heated serving dish. Mix the basil with the cheese and sprinkle over the macaroni. Serve immediately.

From Veneto: _Braised Beef with Polenta (page 31)_

CHEESE AND HAM-STUFFED PASTA

SERVES 6

Known as *panzarotti*, these are a form of ravioli. Here, the filling is made from cheese and ham and the *panzarotti* are deep-fried in contrast to the more customary method of cooking in stock or water.

For the pasta
I egg yolk
2–3 tablespoons milk
100 g/4 oz butter, melted
225 g/8 oz plain flour
½ teaspoon salt
For the filling
225 g/8 oz Mozzarella cheese, finely chopped
50 g/2 oz Parma or Bayonne ham, cut into matchstick strips
25 g/I oz Parmesan cheese, grated
I teaspoon chopped parsley
2 eggs
salt and pepper
2 eggs, beaten, for coating
olive oil for deep frying
I tablespoon chopped parsley to serve

To make the pasta, lightly whisk together the egg yolk, milk and the butter in a small bowl. Sift the flour and salt on to a marble slab or into a mixing bowl and make a well in the centre. Pour in the egg mixture, mix to a firm smooth dough and knead well. Wrap in a damp cloth and set aside for about 30 minutes. Roll the dough into a square 2 mm/$\frac{1}{16}$ in thick. Fold in half, then in half again; repeat four or five times, cover and let stand until required.

To make the filling, mix the Mozzarella, ham, Parmesan cheese and parsley in a bowl. Add the eggs, season with salt and pepper and blend until smooth.

Roll the dough into 2 large sheets, each 3 mm/$\frac{1}{8}$ in thick and brush with a little of the beaten egg. Place small amounts of the filling about 2.5 cm/I in apart on the first sheet of dough. Cover with the second sheet of dough and press firmly around each mound of filling with the fingertips to seal the layers of dough together and completely enclose the filling. Using a serrated pastry wheel or sharp knife, cut the dough into 5-cm/2-in squares. Pinch the edges of the squares together and arrange them on a lightly floured surface so that they do not touch.

Dip the *panzarotti* into the remaining beaten egg and deep fry a few at a time in the hot oil. Remove the *panzarroti* with a perforated spoon after about 5 to 6 minutes when they should be golden brown and crisp. Drain well, and sprinkle lightly with salt. Arrange on a serving dish covered with a doily. Serve immediately, sprinkled with the parsley.

STEAK WITH PIZZAIOLA SAUCE

SERVES 6

(Illustrated on page 37)

Pizzaiola sauce is typically Neapolitan, made from fresh tomatoes and flavoured with garlic and oregano or basil. It is usually served with meat, but it goes well with fish or pasta.

2 tablespoons olive oil
4 sirloin steaks, 1.5 cm/$\frac{3}{4}$ in thick
salt and pepper
3 cloves garlic, peeled and crushed
175 g/6 oz tomatoes, peeled and sliced
pinch of oregano

Heat the olive oil in a heavy frying pan over a high heat. Add the steaks and sauté them on each side until well browned. Reduce the heat and cook them for a further 2 to 3 minutes. Remove the steaks from the frying pan and place on a warmed plate, sprinkle with salt and pepper and keep hot.

Add the garlic to the same frying pan and sauté over a moderate heat until lightly browned. Add the tomatoes and oregano, season with salt and simmer for about 8 minutes, stirring frequently. Return the steaks and the pan juices to the frying pan and simmer for 3 to 4 minutes. Place the steaks on heated plates, pour a little of the sauce over each one, and serve immediately.

TOMATO AND ANCHOVY PIZZA

SERVES 6

According to the historians, pizza originated in the Neolithic Age. With the arrival of tomatoes in the 18th Century, pizza became a dish fit for a king.

25 g/1 oz fresh yeast or 15 g/½ oz dried yeast
300 ml/½ pint lukewarm water
450 g/1 lb plain flour
salt and pepper
1 tablespoon olive oil
75 g/3 oz lard
2 (50-g/2-oz) cans anchovy fillets, drained
350 g/12 oz tomatoes, peeled and sliced
2 cloves garlic, peeled and sliced
½ teaspoon dried oregano

To make the dough, dissolve the yeast in the water. Sift the flour and 1 teaspoon salt into a bowl and make a well in the centre. Pour in the yeast mixture and the olive oil. Knead the flour into the liquid to obtain a smooth dough. Shape it into a ball

From Campania: *Macaroni with Tomato, Ham and Cheese (page 33)*

and put into a floured bowl. Cover and let stand in a warm place for about 1½ to 2 hours, or until doubled in bulk.

Sprinkle the table with a little flour and knead the risen dough for 2 to 3 minutes. Roll out the dough until it is 3 mm/⅛ in thick. Cut it into 6 (15-cm/6-in) circles or one very large circle.

Melt the lard and brush a little over each circle. Arrange the anchovy fillets, tomatoes and garlic over the surface. Sprinkle with the oregano and the remaining melted lard and season with the salt and pepper. Place on a baking sheet and bake in a preheated hot oven (230C, 450F, gas 8) for about 15 to 20 minutes. Serve immediately.

Note In addition to the basic topping ingredients used in this recipe a variety of other foods can be used. Drained canned tomatoes can be used instead of fresh ones. Peeled cooked prawns and shelled cooked mussels can be added. Try sliced salami, ham or pepperoni, sliced mushrooms, capers, olives, chopped basil and cheese. Mozzarella cheese should be thinly sliced and a little grated Parmesan cheese can be added.

TOMATO SAUCE

MAKES ABOUT 450 ml/¾ pint

(Illustrated on page 39)

In this and other regions of Italy, the large juicy tomatoes grow almost anywhere and are one of the most plentiful commodities. Housewives make this sauce in huge quantities every week for use in many varied dishes. To peel tomatoes, submerge them in boiling water for a few minutes. If the tomatoes are ripe, the skins should peel easily.

50 g/2 oz lard
50 g/2 oz ham fat, finely chopped
I clove garlic, peeled and crushed
I medium-sized onion, sliced
I small carrot, sliced
I stick celery, sliced
few sprigs parsley
few sprigs marjoram
I clove
paprika
150 ml/¼ pint white wine
I kg/2 lb ripe tomatoes, peeled,
seeded and chopped
salt

Heat the lard and ham fat in a saucepan over a moderate heat, add the garlic and sauté until lightly browned. Add the onion, carrot, celery, parsley, marjoram, clove and the paprika. Stir together until lightly browned, then pour in the wine. Cook over high heat until the liquid is reduced to I tablespoon. Add the tomatoes and season with salt. Cover the saucepan tightly and simmer over a moderate heat for about I hour, stirring occasionally. If necessary, add a tablespoon of hot water occasionally to prevent the sauce from becoming too thick. Remove the saucepan from the heat and strain the sauce through a fine sieve.

SAVOURY CHEESE AND SALAMI TURNOVERS

MAKES 6 (15-cm/6-in) TURNOVERS

These are known as *calzone* and they are rather like small pizzas, but the dough is folded over to enclose the filling like a pastry. They used to be sold on every street corner and were eaten by farmers and traders alike as they went about their business.

15 g/½ oz fresh yeast
7 g/¼ oz dried yeast
300 ml/½ pint warm water plus
I tablespoon
450 g/I lb plain flour
I teaspoon salt
I tablespoon olive oil
75 g/3 oz lard
350 g/12 oz Mozzarella cheese, thinly
sliced
175 g/6 oz salami, diced
I egg, beaten

Blend the yeast with the water. Sift the flour and salt on to a marble slab or into a mixing bowl and make a well in the centre, and pour in the yeast mixture and the olive oil. Using the fingers, gradually work the flour into the centre, adding the tablespoon of warm water when necessary. Knead until a smooth soft dough is obtained. Form the dough into a ball and place it in a lightly floured bowl. Cover it and let stand in a warm place for about 2 hours, or until doubled in bulk.

Knead the risen dough for 2 to 3 minutes on a floured surface. Roll out the dough to 3 mm/⅛ in thick, cut into 6 15-cm/6-in circles.

Melt the lard and brush a little over each circle. Arrange the cheese and salami over the surface, leaving about I cm/½ in uncovered around the edge. Brush the uncovered edge with the egg. Fold each circle in half, pressing the edges lightly together with the fingertips so that the filling is completely enclosed. Brush the dough with the remaining lard, place on a lightly greased baking sheet and bake in a hot oven (200 C, 400 F, gas 6) for about 20 minutes. Serve immediately.

FRIED SANDWICH

SERVES 6

12 anchovy fillets
6 tablespoons warm milk
6 small, thick slices bread, crusts removed
6 large slices Mozzarella cheese
2 eggs
salt and pepper
flour for coating
olive oil for deep frying

Soak the anchovy fillets in half the milk for 10 to 15 minutes to remove excess salt, then drain them. Sprinkle each slice of bread with a little of the remaining milk. Place 2 anchovy fillets on each slice, then cover with a slice of Mozzarella. Lightly press together to make a neat sandwich.

Lightly beat the eggs with the salt and pepper. Coat the sandwiches on each side with flour, dip them into the egg mixture and coat them again with flour. Heat the oil and deep-fry the sandwiches until golden brown. Drain well on absorbent kitchen paper and serve immediately.

From Campania: *Steak with Pizzaiola Sauce (page 34)*

VERMICELLI WITH TOMATO SAUCE

SERVES 6

1 tablespoon chopped onion
75 g/3 oz butter
225 g/8 oz tomatoes, peeled and sliced
salt and pepper
450 g/1 lb vermicelli
1–2 tablespoons chopped fresh basil
100 g/4 oz Parmesan cheese, grated

Fry onion in some butter, then add the tomatoes, Season, lower the heat, and simmer for 15 minutes, stirring occasionally.

Cook the vermicelli rapidly in lightly salted boiling water for 3 to 5 minutes, or until *al dente* (cooked but still firm). Drain and place in a heated deep serving dish. Dot with the remaining butter and pour over the sauce. Sprinkle with the basil and some of the cheese. Serve the remaining cheese separately.

Apulia to Calabria

From the east of Italy across the southern-most coast to the west, here are the dishes from Apulia, Lucania and Calabria.

In this part of the world, the tourist industry is the main means of support, mainly due to the many days of sunshine every year.

A large amount of vegetables are grown here, including artichokes, asparagus, aubergines, celery, sweet peppers and tomatoes. There is a lot of game and pigs and goats are reared domestically.

The Ionian sea produces excellent oysters, mussels and other fish which are used extensively in hot-pots along with wine and garlic. A variety of sausages are also available and Lucania is noted for this.

The region produces no really great cheeses, but a range of good ones. There are many versions of Pecorino, a hard ewe's milk cheese which is used a great deal in cooking. Genuine Mozzarella and Provola cheeses are produced in Apulia and Calabria.

Apulia was one of the first Italian provinces to produce wine, in quantity if not in quality! San Severo, which is either white or red, is an above average local table wine. Most Apulian wines are used in the manufacture of Vermouth. Calabria produces some trustworthy reds, among which should be mentioned Ciro, which is rather sweet, and Lacrima di Castrovillari, which is rather dry.

FRIED SWEET PEPPERS AND TOMATOES

SERVES 6

(Illustrated on page 13)

In Italy vegetables are rarely served as an accompaniment to meat; usually a green salad is considered sufficient. A vegetable dish such as this one is served in its own right as a first course before the meat.

6 tablespoons olive oil
1 large onion, coarsely chopped
2–3 cloves garlic, peeled
6 small bay leaves
1 kg/2 lb red, yellow or green sweet peppers, deseeded and chopped
salt and pepper
675 g/1½ lb fresh tomatoes, peeled, or 2 (425-g/15-oz) cans tomatoes

Heat the olive oil in a saucepan over a moderate heat. Add the onion, garlic and bay leaves and sauté until golden brown. Add the sweet peppers and season with salt and pepper. Cook over a high heat for about 10 minutes, stirring constantly. Add the tomatoes, lower the heat and simmer gently for a further 15 minutes. Pour into a heated serving dish and serve immediately.

Note This dish may be reheated very successfully and therefore can be prepared in advance when entertaining.

From Campania: *Tomato Sauce (page 36)*

MUSSELS WITH WHITE WINE AND GARLIC

SERVES 6

3.5 litres/6 pints mussels
5 tablespoons olive oil
6 cloves garlic, peeled and sliced
½ chilli, deseeded and chopped
250 ml/8 fl oz dry white wine
I tablespoon chopped parsley

Scrape and wash the mussels thoroughly under cold running water. Remove and discard the beards. Discard any shellfish which are open and do not shut when sharply tapped.

Heat the olive oil in a large saucepan, add the garlic and chilli and sauté until browned. Add the mussels with the wine and the parsley. Cover the pan and bring to the boil, then reduce the heat.

Simmer until the mussels have all opened, shaking the pan frequently. Add a few tablespoons of warm water, if necessary, to prevent the mussels from sticking. Discard any mussels which have not opened, then ladle them into individual bowls and serve immediately.

FRICASSÉE OF LAMB

SERVES 6

2 tablespoons olive oil
I kg/2 lb boned leg or shoulder of
lamb, cubed
I small onion, chopped
50 g/2 oz uncooked ham, minced
pinch of ground nutmeg
salt and pepper
150 ml/¼ pint dry white wine
15 g/½ oz plain flour
2 cloves garlic, peeled and chopped
2 tablespoons chopped parsley
4 egg yolks
2 tablespoons lemon juice

Heat the olive oil in a flameproof casserole, add the lamb, onion, ham, nutmeg and seasoning. Stir until the meat begins to brown, add the wine and reduce it over a high heat until there is only I tablespoon of liquid. Stir in the flour and enough water to barely cover the lamb. Simmer over a low heat for 50 to 60 minutes. During cooking, add a few tablespoons water if the liquid has dried up, to prevent the meat from sticking. Combine the garlic and parsley. Stir in the garlic mixture 2 to 3 minutes before the end of cooking time. Remove the casserole from the heat.

Lightly beat the egg yolks with the lemon juice. Stir this mixture into the contents of the casserole. Put the casserole back on the heat until the mixture is hot and the sauce thickens but make sure it does not boil or it will curdle. Remove the casserole from the heat immediately and pour the fricassée into a deep warmed serving dish. Serve immediately.

LAMB STEW

SERVES 6

(Illustrated on page 43)
This dish is typical of Italy and the whole Mediterranean area.

I tablespoon olive oil
I kg/2 lb shoulder of lamb, cubed
100 g/4 oz bacon fat, chopped
½ small carrot, chopped
½ onion, chopped
I clove garlic, peeled and chopped
I stick celery, finely chopped
150 ml/¼ pint dry white wine
⅓ quantity Tomato Sauce (page 36)
150 ml/¼ pint water
salt
¼ teaspoon chilli powder
350 g/12 oz potatoes, peeled, cubed
and parboiled

Heat the olive oil in a flameproof casserole, add the lamb and sauté until browned. Remove the lamb and set aside.

Cook the bacon fat, carrot, onion, garlic and celery in the remaining oil until browned. Pour in the wine and reduce it to 3 tablespoons over a high heat. Add the tomato sauce and the water, season with salt and the chilli powder. Simmer for 15 minutes. Return the lamb to the casserole and simmer for a further 20 to 30 minutes, stirring frequently. Add the potatoes about 10 minutes before the end of the cooking time.

From Apulia to Calabria: *Mussels with White Wine and Garlic*.

Sicily & Sardinia

These are the largest islands in the Mediterranean, and they have in common a rich cuisine that displays the influence of successive waves of Phoenicians, Greeks, Carthaginians, Romans, Arabs, and Normans. Thus you will find couscous, a typically North African concoction of crushed grain and mutton or chicken, on the same menu as Greek or Turkish style dishes, and Italian pasta.

Pasta, in fact, is said to have originated in Sicily in the early 13th Century. Certainly great quantities are eaten there, particularly in the form of lasagne, coloured green with spinach. In Sardinia in particular, superb homemade bread is often substituted for pasta.

Both islands have superb fish recipes and tuna fish is served in a dozen ingenious ways. There are also many good vegetable dishes, and aubergines are stuffed and cooked in many different ways. Oranges and lemons grow abundantly in Sicily and form the fruity basis of many ice creams, in the manufacture of which the islanders dispute pride of place with the Neapolitans. Cassata was invented in Sicily.

Among Sicilian wines, the best known must be Marsala, a rich brown sweet wine, which was created by an Englishman as a rival to Madeira. It is much used in the kitchen, for cooking kidneys and veal and, of course, in the preparation of zabaione.

AUBERGINES WITH BLACK OLIVES AND TOMATOES

SERVES 8

(Illustrated on page 45)

The region of origin of this dish is disputed but many claim that it was created in Sicily. It is important to use a good quality white wine vinegar to appreciate the delicate flavour of the vegetables.

450 g/ 1 lb large, round aubergines
salt and pepper
3 tablespoons cold water
150 ml/¼ pint olive oil
1 large onion, thinly sliced
6 sticks celery, blanched in boiling, salted water and sliced
175 g/ 6 oz black olives, stoned
450 g/ 1 lb tomatoes, peeled and chopped
2 tablespoons capers
1 tablespoon pine kernels
150 ml/¼ pint white wine vinegar
25 g/ 1 oz caster sugar

Dice the unskinned aubergines into 1-cm/½-in cubes and place them in a bowl. Sprinkle them with ½ teaspoon of salt and the water and set aside for 30 minutes. Drain them well and rinse them under cold running water. Squeeze lightly to remove the excess moisture, and dry thoroughly with a cloth or kitchen paper.

Heat half the olive oil in a frying pan over a moderate heat, add the aubergines, season lightly with salt and pepper and sauté them until well browned. Remove the aubergines with a perforated spoon, drain and set aside.

Pour any olive oil from the frying pan and the remaining olive oil into a saucepan. Add the onion and cook over a low heat until soft, but not browned. Add the aubergines, celery and the olives. Mix well, then stir in the tomatoes. Season with a pinch of salt and simmer for about 10 to 15 minutes. Add the capers, pine kernels, vinegar and the sugar. Cover and simmer for a further 15 minutes, or until the celery is tender, stirring frequently. Pour into a serving bowl. Serve cold.

From Apulia to Calabria: _Lamb Stew (page 40)_

CHEESE-STUFFED POTATO PASTA

SERVES 8

Sardinia, invaded by the Phoenicians before the time of Christ, assimilated the finer arts of cooking from the conquerors into their everyday fare.

1.5 kg/3 lb potatoes
6 eggs, beaten
175 g/6 oz butter, softened
2 tablespoons olive oil
450 g/1 lb onions, finely chopped
1 tablespoon chopped mint
100 g/4 oz Pecorino cheese, grated
1 egg, beaten with 2 teaspoons water
$\frac{1}{2}$ quantity Tomato Sauce (page 36)
extra grated Pecorino cheese, to
serve (optional)

Place the potatoes in lightly salted boiling water and simmer until tender. Drain well and cool slightly. Remove the skin and press the potatoes through a sieve into a bowl, or put them through a potato ricer. Add the eggs and butter and mix to a smooth dough. Leave covered for 30 minutes.

To make the filling, heat the olive oil in a small saucepan, add the onions and sauté them until soft but not browned. Remove the saucepan from the heat and add the mint and cheese. Cool the mixture slightly, then put it into a piping bag fitted with a large plain nozzle.

Roll out the dough into 2 sheets 2 mm/$\frac{1}{16}$in thick. Brush the sheets with the egg beaten with water. Pipe small amounts of filling about 3.5–5 cm/1$\frac{1}{2}$–2 in apart on to the first sheet. Cover with the second sheet and press firmly around each mound of filling with the fingertips to seal the layers of dough together to completely enclose the filling. Sprinkle a 5-cm/2-in pastry cutter or a sharp knife with flour; cut out the pasta into circles or 5-cm/2-in squares.

Arrange the squares on a lightly floured surface so that they do not touch. Drop the pasta, a few at a time, into a saucepan half-filled with lightly salted, boiling water and simmer for about 5 minutes. Remove with a perforated spoon when they rise to the surface. Drain them well and layer them in a heated serving dish with the tomato sauce and additional cheese, if liked, between the layers. Serve very hot.

ROLLED BEEF BRAISED IN RED WINE

SERVES 6

The meticulous and painstaking Sicilian cook takes great pride in preparing this speciality which requires considerable care and exact timing to produce a perfect result.

1 kg/2 lb rump steak in 1 large slice
salt and pepper
4 hard-boiled eggs
175 g/6 oz soft Caciotta or Mozzarella cheese
100 g/4 oz minced ham, lean rindless bacon or sausagemeat
3 cloves garlic, peeled and chopped
1 tablespoon chopped parsley
pinch of oregano
salt and pepper
1 tablespoon olive oil
1 small onion, coarsely chopped
1 medium-sized carrot, sliced
1 bay leaf
3–4 tablespoons beef stock or water
5 tablespoons dry red wine

Place the beef on a chopping board and beat it with a meat mallet or a wooden rolling pin until it is about 1 cm/$\frac{1}{2}$ in thick. Season with salt and pepper and set aside.

To make the stuffing, slice the eggs and cheese and mix them with the ham, bacon or sausagemeat. Add 1 clove of the garlic, parsley and the oregano to the egg mixture. Season with salt and pepper. Spread the stuffing over the beef and roll it up tightly to completely enclose it. Secure it with fine string and season with salt and pepper. Brush the beef thoroughly with olive oil and place in a well-greased casserole. Place the onion, carrot, the rest of the garlic and the bay leaf around the beef. Add the stock and place in a preheated, moderately hot oven (190 C, 375 F, gas 5) and cook for about 1 hour, basting occasionally.

When cooked, remove the string, slice the beef and place on a heated serving dish. Add the wine to the remaining juices, reduce to 2 tablespoons in a saucepan over a high heat and strain the liquid over the meat. Serve immediately.

SICILIAN RICE CROQUETTES

MAKES ABOUT 20

Rice is not used as much in Sicily as in other parts of Italy, although it was introduced into Italy through Sicily by the Arabs. This recipe is for a traditional rice snack from the island.

5 tablespoons olive oil
1 small onion, finely chopped
225 g/8 oz chicken liver, lamb's sweetbreads and minced lean veal, in equal quantities
salt and pepper
5 tablespoons dry white wine
15 g/$\frac{1}{2}$ oz plain flour
4 tablespoons vegetable stock or water
450 g/1 lb Italian rice (or other long-grain rice)
100 g/4 oz plain flour
2 eggs, beaten
100 g/4 oz breadcrumbs
about 300 ml/$\frac{1}{2}$ pint oil for deep-frying

Heat the olive oil in a saucepan over a moderate heat and add the onion and sauté until lightly browned. Mince the liver, sweetbreads and veal and add this to the onion. Season with salt and pepper and simmer for about 5 minutes. Pour in the wine and reduce on high heat to 1 teaspoon. Sprinkle with the flour and cook, stirring occasionally, until browned. Add the stock and bring to the boil over a moderate heat, stirring constantly until the sauce is well cooked and quite thick. Remove the saucepan from the heat and set it aside to cool.

Cook the rice in plenty of boiling, salted water for 18 to 20 minutes, or until it is *al dente* (cooked but still firm). Drain the rice and place on a table or a large tray, spreading it with a wooden spoon to prevent it from sticking together. When the rice is cold, wet your hands, and form the rice into balls, about 5 cm/2 in. in diameter. Make a depression in the middle of each ball with the finger. Fill each depression with a little of the giblet mixture, then press the rice over the filling to completely seal it. Coat the balls with flour then with the beaten egg and then the breadcrumbs. Deep fry them a few at a time in the hot oil, until crisp and well-browned. Drain and serve immediately.

SICILIAN PASTRY HORNS

SERVES 6

These Sicilian pastries are rather like cream horns, but they are fried. Marsala, the famous Sicilian wine, gives the pastry a delicate unusual fragrance.

For the pastry
350 g/ 12 oz plain flour
pinch of salt
150 ml/¼ pint plus 3 tablespoons
Marsala
pinch of caster sugar
oil for deep frying
For the filling
25 g/ 1 oz pistachio nuts, chopped
25 g/ 1 oz mixed candied peel,
chopped
450 g/ 1 lb ricotta cheese
225 g/ 8 oz caster sugar
about 100 g/ 4 oz sifted icing sugar to
decorate

Sift the flour and salt on to a marble slab or into a mixing bowl and make a well in the centre. Pour in

From Sicily and Sardinia: *Aubergines with Black Olives and Tomatoes (page 42)*

the Marsala, add the sugar and mix to a firm dough. Knead well until smooth, cover with a damp cloth and set aside for about 2 hours.

Roll out the dough into sheets about 3 mm/⅛ in thick, and cut it into 10-cm/4-in squares. Roll each square around a metal cream horn or cornet mould, about 10 cm/4 in long, and set aside for about 30 minutes.

Heat the oil in a deep fryer and add the pastry-covered moulds. Remove them when golden-brown and drain well. Place them on a cloth to cool slightly. Slide the pastry cases carefully off the moulds and leave them until they are cold.

To make the filling, combine the pistachio nuts, candied peel, cheese and sugar. Place the filling in a piping bag with a large plain nozzle. Fill the pastry horns with the cheese filling and dust them with icing sugar.

Liguria

Liguria is the smallest province in Italy, found in the north of the country. Its chief city is Genoa, which has been a flourishing seaport for more than a thousand years. The cooking of the region makes abundant use of the local olive oil, which is claimed with some justice to be one of the best in Italy.

Pesto is one of the best sauces to accompany pasta. It is made from basil, garlic, cheese, and olive oil. It is said in Genoa that only locally-grown basil imparts the authentic tang. Pesto is frequently served with soup, fish, and meat. The Ligurian cuisine has much in common with the southern French, using fish in stews flavoured with garlic, onions, and herbs.

Characteristically, Ligurian dishes have long and complex lists of ingredients. For example, turkey is boiled in a soup that contains onion, celery, parsley, carrots, bay leaves, sage, rosemary, thyme, cloves, nutmeg, and truffles!

The wines of the region are not outstanding in quality and neither are they very numerous. Perhaps the best come from the Cinque Terre region near La Spezia. Sciacchetra is a rather sweet and heavy dessert wine. The other noteworthy wines are also white, but without exception extremely dry. Names to look out for are Coronato, Conigliano, and Polcevera. A good grappa is distilled from grape pressings in the town of Chiavari.

NOODLES WITH PESTO

SERVES 6

Tagliatelle made its first appearance at a dinner in honour of Lucrezia Borgia. The cook was inspired by her long blonde hair and devised these light ribbon-like noodles.

5 eggs
1 tablespoon olive oil
450 g/1 lb plain flour
1 teaspoon salt
350 g/12 oz potatoes, peeled and thinly sliced
50 g/2 oz Pecorino cheese, grated
1 quantity Pesto (page 53)

Lightly whisk the eggs and olive oil in a small bowl. Sift the flour and salt on to a marble slab or into a mixing bowl and make a well in the centre. Pour in the egg mixture. Mix to a firm dough and knead well. Wrap the dough in a damp cloth and set aside for about 30 minutes.

Roll the dough into sheets, about 2 mm/$\frac{1}{16}$ in thick. Fold each sheet in half lengthways, then fold it in half lengthways again, and again. With a sharp knife, cut the dough into noodles, 2.5 cm/1 in wide. Unfold the noodles and place them on a floured surface. Cover with a lightly floured cloth and set aside for at least 15 minutes.

Simmer the potatoes in lightly salted boiling water until they are almost cooked. Add the noodles and continue simmering until they are *al dente* (cooked but still firm). Drain the noodles and potatoes and reserve 2 tablespoons of the liquid.

Place the noodles and potatoes on an oval heated serving dish. Sprinkle them with the cheese and the reserved cooking liquid and mix lightly. Pour the *Pesto* over the mixture and bring to the table. Mix together until the potatoes and noodles are well coated and serve immediately.

RAVIOLI GENOESE STYLE

SERVES 6

It is said that ravioli was invented on sailing ships in the days when fresh foods were scarce. All leftovers were chopped and wrapped in dough to be cooked for the next meal. This was called *raviole*, meaning something of no value.

2 eggs
300 ml/½ pint warm water
1 teaspoon olive oil
575 g/ 1¼ lb plain flour
1 teaspoon salt
For the filling
50 g/2 oz butter
450 g/ 1 lb minced veal
225 g/8 oz calf's brains
225 g/8 oz calf's sweetbreads
100 g/4 oz beetroot leaves or spinach, chopped
1 slice white bread, crusts removed
40 g/1½ oz Parmesan cheese, grated
7 eggs
4 egg yolks
salt
¾ quantity Meat Sauce (page 64)
or
1 quantity Mushroom Sauce (page 52) or
1 quantity Pesto (page 53)
extra Parmesan cheese, grated to serve

To make the pasta, lightly whisk together the eggs, water and olive oil in a small bowl. Sift the flour and salt onto a marble slab or into a mixing bowl and make a well in the centre. Pour in the egg mixture, mix to a firm smooth dough and knead well. Wrap the dough in a damp cloth and set aside for about 30 minutes.

To make the filling, heat the butter in a frying pan over a moderate heat and sauté the veal for 5 to 10 minutes, or until well browned. Set aside until required. Soak the brains and sweetbreads in cold water for 1 hour. Blanch the brains and sweetbreads in boiling water for 10 minutes. Drain them well and remove any membranes, blood vessels and gristle. Soak the bread in a little cold water for about 1 minute, then squeeze to remove the excess water.

Mince the brains and sweetbreads several times until very fine. Add the veal, beetroot leaves or

From Liguria: *Noodles with Pesto (opposite)*

spinach, bread, cheese, 6 of the eggs, egg yolks, and salt to taste and mix to a paste. With floured fingers, roll the mixture into balls about the size of a walnut and set aside on a floured surface.

Roll the dough into 2 sheets, about 2 mm/1/16 in thick. Beat the remaining egg and brush the first sheet with it. Arrange the small balls of filling on the brushed sheet of dough about 2.5–3.5 cm/ 1–1½ in apart. Cover with the second sheet of dough and press firmly around each ball of filling with the fingertips to seal the layers of dough together and completely enclose the filling. With a serrated pastry wheel or a sharp knife, cut out the ravioli squares and arrange them on a lightly floured surface so that they do not touch.

Place a few ravioli at a time in a large saucepan, half-filled with lightly salted, boiling water. Simmer for about 5 minutes, remove them with a perforated spoon as they float to the surface. Drain them thoroughly.

Arrange the ravioli on an oval, heated serving dish in layers, spooning the meat sauce, mushroom sauce, or *Pesto* between the layers. Serve immediately with the cheese.

STUFFED LETTUCE

SERVES 6

Pecorino and Parmesan are the two most widely used cheeses in Italy and they are fairly similar in texture. Pecorino, a hard, sharp cheese originally made with whole sheep's milk, is made to many local recipes around the country and therefore varies slightly from region to region.

100 g/4 oz lamb's or calf's brains
½ lemon
100 g/4 oz lamb's or calf's sweetbreads
12 medium-sized heads of lettuce
450 g/1 lb fillet of veal
75–100 g/3–4 oz butter
½ bay leaf
salt
1 clove garlic, peeled and chopped
few sprigs marjoram
pinch of ground nutmeg
100 g/4 oz Pecorino or Parmesan cheese, grated
2 eggs
1 egg yolk
salt and pepper
2 litres/3½ pints good beef stock

Soak the brains in cold water for about 1 hour. Drain them well and dry them with a clean cloth or kitchen paper. Rub the surface of the brains with the cut side of the lemon, then replace them in cold water and soak until they become very white. Soak the sweetbreads in warm water for 10 to 15 minutes.

Remove and discard the coarse outer leaves of each lettuce, retaining the hearts. Rinse the hearts under cold running water and blanch in boiling water for 3 minutes. Drain well and stand upside-down on a plate, to allow more moisture to drain away.

Trim any membrane, gristle and fat from the veal and cut the meat into very thin small slices. Heat the butter in a frying pan over a moderate heat. Add the veal, bay leaf and salt and sauté, stirring frequently, for 15 to 20 minutes or until the veal is tender. Remove the pan from the heat, drain the veal, reserve the juices and set aside to cool.

Drain the brains and sweetbreads and rinse them under cold running water. Blanch them in boiling water for 10 minutes. Drain them well and remove any membrane, blood vessels and gristle. Reheat the reserved juices in the frying pan. Add the brains and sweetbreads and simmer for 15 to 20 minutes, or until they are tender. Remove the frying pan from the heat, remove the brains and sweetbreads and set aside until cool. Coarsely chop the brains, sweetbreads and veal; place them in a bowl. Add the garlic, marjoram, nutmeg, 1 tablespoon of the cheese, the eggs, egg yolk and salt and pepper to taste. Open each lettuce heart and stuff it with the mixture. Very carefully tie each heart with thread to avoid losing the filling during cooking.

Pour the beef stock into a large saucepan and bring it to the boil over a high heat. Carefully lower the lettuce hearts into the pan, bring to the boil again, reduce the heat and simmer very gently for about 15 minutes. Remove from the heat, carefully take out the hearts and remove and discard the thread. Drain them for about 1 minute, then place them on a heated serving dish. Serve immediately with the remaining grated cheese.

FILLET OF VEAL IN WHITE WINE

SERVES 6

In Italy, this dish is cooked in a *tegame*, a round double-handled aluminium pan; a frying pan can be used instead. Ideally, milk-fed veal should be used.

450 g/1 lb fillet of veal
salt and pepper
50 g/2 oz butter
1 tablespoon oil
2 bay leaves
5 tablespoons dry white wine

Cut the veal into 5-mm × 7.5-cm/¼-in × 3-in slices and season with salt and pepper. Heat the butter and oil in a frying pan over a moderate heat. Add the bay leaves and lightly sauté them for 1 minute. Increase the heat, add the veal and sauté on each side for 3 to 4 minutes, or until golden brown. Reduce the heat and cook for a further 1 minute.

Arrange the veal slices on a heated serving dish and keep hot. Add the wine to the juices left in the frying pan, reduce it over high heat to 2 tablespoons of liquid. Pour this over the veal. Serve hot, with vegetables. Artichokes are an especially suitable accompaniment.

GNOCCHI WITH PESTO

SERVES 6

1.75 kg/4 lb large potatoes
salt
350 g/12 oz plain flour
1 tablespoon grated Pecorino cheese
2 tablespoons fine fresh breadcrumbs
25 g/1 oz butter
4 egg yolks (optional)
1 quantity Pesto (page 53)

Place the unpeeled potatoes in a saucepan and cover with lightly salted cold water. Place the saucepan over a moderate heat and bring to the boil. Simmer until barely tender.

Meanwhile, mix together the flour, cheese, breadcrumbs, butter and 1 teaspoon salt. Drain and peel the potatoes, press through a sieve onto a marble slab or into a mixing bowl.

While the potatoes are still warm, make a well in the centre and add the flour mixture and egg yolks. Mix to a soft dough, adding a little more flour, if necessary. Knead lightly until smooth, then divide the dough into pieces and, with floured hands,

From Liguria: *Fillet of Veal in White Wine (opposite)*

shape it into long rolls, about 2.5 cm/1 in. in diameter. Cut the rolls into 3.5-cm/1½-in pieces and make a lengthways groove on either side of each piece by pressing it between the index and second fingers. Arrange the pieces on a lightly floured surface, making sure they do not touch. Set aside for 10 to 15 minutes to dry.

Half fill a large saucepan with lightly salted, boiling water. Place a few of the gnocchi at a time into the pan. As they come to the surface, remove them with a perforated spoon. Drain them well and place them on a large, heated serving dish. Heat the *Pesto*, pour it over the gnocchi with 2 tablespoons of the cooking liquid and stir to mix. Serve immediately.

STUFFED VEAL

SERVES 6

Traditionally known as *cima*, this stuffed breast of veal is flattened to its characteristic shape by placing a wooden board on top of the cooked meat and weighing it down, using heavy iron weights. It is usually served cold, but can also be reheated and served hot.

1.25 kg/2½ lb boned breast of veal
225 g/8 oz white bread, crusts removed
300 ml/½ pint milk
450 g/1 lb pork fillet or fillet of veal, minced
100 g/4 oz bacon fat, minced
2 tablespoons chopped fresh marjoram or
3 teaspoons dried marjoram
40 g/1½ oz Parmesan cheese, grated
225 g/8 oz shelled peas, Swiss chard or beetroot leaves, coarsely chopped
50 g/2 oz pistachio nuts, chopped
4 eggs
pinch of ground nutmeg
salt and pepper
1 medium-sized onion, sliced
1 small carrot, sliced
½ bay leaf
2 peppercorns
salt

Cut a slit at one end of the veal, insert a long sharp knife through the slit and cut the inside of the veal to make a 'pocket' to hold the stuffing.

To make the stuffing, soak the bread in the milk, then squeeze out the excess moisture. Place the bread, pork fillet, bacon fat, marjoram, cheese, peas, pistachio nuts, eggs, nutmeg and salt and pepper in a bowl and mix to form a paste.

Press the stuffing into the veal and sew up the slit with thread. Loosely tie the veal with thin string, so that it maintains its shape when cooking. Place the veal in a flameproof casserole or large saucepan and cover with plenty of cold water. Add the onion, carrot and bay leaf, peppercorns and salt. Place over a moderate heat and bring to the boil. Lower the heat and simmer, partially covered, for 2 hours or until the veal is tender.

Remove the veal from the liquid and place it on a flat surface. Reserve the liquid for soup stock if desired. Put weights on the veal to press it. Leave it for 2 hours or until cold. Serve cold.

VEAL IN WINE SAUCE

SERVES 6

Dried mushrooms, sometimes imported from the Orient, strung on string like necklaces, have a strong and amazingly fresh flavour. Fresh mushrooms are a very poor substitute.

450 g/1 lb lean boneless veal, cut from the leg
salt and freshly milled black pepper
50 g/2 oz butter
2 tablespoons olive oil
½ small onion, finely chopped
1 small carrot, finely chopped
6 dried mushrooms, soaked and drained or
6 fresh mushrooms, finely chopped
1 clove
½ bay leaf
5 tablespoons dry white wine
1 teaspoon plain flour
450 g/1 lb tomatoes, peeled and finely chopped
3 tablespoons warm water

Tie the veal with fine string to maintain its shape and season with salt and pepper. Heat the butter and olive oil in a large saucepan over a high heat, add the veal and sauté until browned. Add the onion, carrot, mushrooms, clove and bay leaf and sauté until lightly browned. Pour the wine over the veal and simmer until it is reduced to 2 tablespoons. Lower the heat and stir in the flour. When it becomes brown, add the tomatoes and warm water and adjust the seasoning.

Cover the saucepan tightly and simmer for about 1 hour over a moderate heat, adding more warm water if the sauce thickens too much. Remove the veal from the saucepan. Discard the string and place the veal on a heated serving plate. Strain the sauce through a fine sieve and pour it over the veal. Serve immediately.

BAKED RICE WITH MUSHROOMS AND FRESH PEAS

SERVES 6

Italy is Europe's largest producer of rice and the crop has been cultivated since the 16th Century, although rice appeared on the tables of the wealthy from as early as the 12th Century.

100 g/4 oz butter
1 small onion, chopped
225 g/8 oz sausagemeat
salt and pepper
675 g/ 1½ lb small fresh peas, shelled
6 dried mushrooms, soaked and drained or
6 fresh mushrooms, coarsely chopped
½ filoni (long Italian loaf), cubed
300 ml/½ pint beef roast gravy
450 g/1 lb Italian rice (or other long-grain rice)
1.15 litres/2 pints beef stock or water
100 g/4 oz Parmesan cheese, grated

From Liguria: *Easter Pie (overleaf)*

Heat one-third of the butter in a saucepan over a moderate heat and add the onion and sauté until lightly browned. Add the sausagemeat and salt and pepper and mix lightly. Add the peas, mushrooms and bread cubes and continue cooking for 5 to 10 minutes, stirring frequently. Stir in the gravy and bring the mixture to the boil. Stir in the rice and add the stock gradually as the rice absorbs the liquid. Simmer for about 10 to 12 minutes, or until the rice is *al dente* (cooked but still firm). Remove the saucepan from the heat and blend in the remaining butter and half the cheese.

Pour the mixture into an ovenproof casserole and smooth the top with the back of a spoon. Place in a moderately hot oven (200C, 400F, gas 6) and bake for 15 to 20 minutes, or until a golden brown crust forms on top. Serve immediately with the remaining cheese.

EASTER PIE

SERVES 6

(Illustrated on previous page)

This traditional cheese and spinach pie is reminiscent of the Balkan cheese pies. The pastry takes some time to prepare but the effort is rewarded in the delicious and very attractive result.

1 kg/2 lb plain flour
1½ teaspoons salt
1 tablespoon olive oil
600 ml/1 pint water
100 g/4 oz spinach or young small-veined beetroot leaves, finely shredded
50 g/2 oz Parmesan cheese, grated
1½ teaspoons chopped fresh marjoram and parsley or 1 teaspoon dried marjoram and parsley
350 g/12 oz ricotta cheese
15 g/½ oz plain flour
3 tablespoons single cream
salt and freshly ground black pepper
2 tablespoons olive oil
6 eggs
50 g/2 oz melted butter

Sift the flour and salt onto a marble slab or into a mixing bowl and make a well in the centre. Pour in the olive oil and water and mix to a very soft dough. Knead well and divide into 10 pieces, place the pieces on a floured cloth and cover with a damp cloth.

Cook the spinach or beetroot leaves in lightly salted, boiling water for 8 to 10 minutes. Drain the leaves, squeeze them to remove the excess moisture, and spread them on a large plate. Sprinkle with half the Parmesan cheese and the marjoram and parsley.

Blend the ricotta cheese with the 15 g/½ oz flour and press through a sieve into a bowl. Add the cream and the salt and pepper. Roll out 5 pieces of the dough into very thin sheets, each about 33 cm/13 in. in diameter. Place in layers in a 30-cm/12-in cake tin or deep pie dish, brushing each layer with 2 tablespoons olive oil, except the last one. Carefully press them firmly against the bottom and the sides of the tin. Spread the leaves evenly over the top layer of dough. Sprinkle with olive oil and cover with the ricotta mixture.

With the back of a spoon, make 6 hollows in the cheese mixture and carefully crack 1 egg into each one, without breaking the yolks. Pour a little of the melted butter over each egg, season with salt and pepper to taste and the remaining Parmesan cheese.

Roll out the remaining pieces of dough to the same size as the other pieces. Layer them over the mixture, brushing each one with oil. Trim off any dough overlapping the edge of the flan tin. Make a braid with these trimmings and place it round the edge of the pie.

Brush the surface of the dough with oil and lightly prick it with a fork to allow the steam to escape during cooking, taking care not to break the egg yolks. Place in a preheated, moderately hot oven (190C, 375F, gas 5) and bake for 50 to 60 minutes. Easter pie is excellent eaten hot or cold.

MUSHROOM SAUCE

MAKES ABOUT 450 ml/¾ pint

The ancients believed that fungi were spawned by bolts of lightning. The Romans delighted in mushrooms but many, to their cost, were unable to distinguish between the edible and lethal varieties. The garlic is used to enhance the mushroom flavour, but it is discarded before the sauce becomes excessively impregnated.

5 tablespoons olive oil
4 cloves garlic, peeled
450 g/1 lb fresh mushrooms, thinly sliced
1 tablespoon chopped parsley
450 g/1 lb tomatoes, peeled and chopped
150 ml/¼ pint warm water
salt and freshly milled black pepper

Heat the olive oil in a frying pan over a moderate heat. Sauté the garlic until lightly browned and then discard it. Add the mushrooms and parsley and sauté for 2 minutes. Add the tomatoes, water and season with salt and pepper. Cover tightly and simmer the mixture over a moderate heat for about 20 minutes, stirring occasionally and adding a little more water, if necessary.

PESTO

MAKES ABOUT 150 ml/¼ pint

Pesto is the traditional sauce of Genoa. The ingredients are placed in a mortar and pounded with a pestle (hence the name) without mercy until the result is a smooth aromatic paste. Basil can be seen everywhere in Genoa, tended with loving care by the housewives. Although _Pesto_ in its original form is made with basil only, it may be made using spinach, marjoram and parsley, as in this recipe.

> I large bunch fresh basil
> few spinach leaves (optional)
> few sprigs parsley (optional)
> few sprigs marjoram (optional)
> 3 cloves garlic, peeled
> pinch of coarse salt
> 75–100 g/3–4 oz Pecorino cheese,
> grated
> 5 tablespoons olive oil
> 1–2 tablespoons water

Remove the stalks from the basil and clean it well with a cloth without washing it. Clean the spinach, parsley and marjoram, if used, in a similar manner. Gradually add the basil, spinach, parsley, marjoram, garlic and the salt to a large mortar or a bowl, while pounding the mixture carefully, stirring it occasionally, until it is reduced to a smooth pulp. Add the cheese and pound to a well-blended paste.

Add the oil, drop by drop, beating constantly, as if making a mayonnaise. Blend the liquid into the paste until smooth, adding the water. This water should preferably be pasta cooking water.

Note If _Pesto_ is made in a larger quantity, it may be stored in jars, covered with a layer of olive oil, and used as required.

From Emilia-Romagna: _Cheese-stuffed Pasta in Broth (overleaf)_

Emilia-Romagna

The twin provinces of Emilia and Romagna, east of the Apennines and south of the River Po, form the heartland of classic Italian gastronomy. Here are Parma, famous for its ham and cheese, and Bologna, renowned for its sauce. Here, the best pork in Italy is raised and the best pasta in the world is cooked. The region's sausages alone would entitle it to culinary fame: cotechino *is a speciality of Modena and* mortadella *is the famous Bologna sausage.*

When correctly made, Bolognese sauce (or ragù as the inhabitants of Bologna perversely call it) is the best of all accompaniments to pasta. This region is also famous for prosciutto, a ham which is often served raw with such fruit as melon or figs, but is sometimes tossed in butter and eaten with spaghetti, and the expensive but highly prized culatello di zibello, *cured pork butt steeped in white wine.*

The region's bakers maintain a high standard. The bread is as good as anywhere in Europe, and there is the widest possible range of little cakes and gâteaux, for which the town of Parma is particularly noted.

The wine of Emilia and Romagna fall short of excellence, but cannot be bettered as honest table wines. Notable is Lambrusco, an unusual sparkling wine that can be either sweet or dry, red or white. Albana is a dessert wine of some charm.

CHEESE-STUFFED PASTA IN BROTH

SERVES 6

(Illustrated on previous page)

These little stuffed pasta are known as *cappelletti*, meaning 'little hats', and they appear throughout northern Italy with a variety of fillings. This mixed cheese stuffing is typical of Emilia-Romagna.

For the pasta
4 eggs
2 teaspoons olive oil
350g/12oz plain flour
¾ teaspoon salt
For the filling
175g/6oz ricotta cheese
25g/1oz Parmesan cheese, grated
1 egg
1 egg yolk
¼ teaspoon grated lemon rind
pinch of mixed dried herbs
salt
2.5 litres/4¼ pints beef or chicken broth
100g/4oz Parmesan cheese, grated

To make the pasta, lightly whisk the eggs and olive oil in a small bowl. Sift the flour and salt on to a marble slab or into a mixing bowl and make a well in the centre. Pour in the eggs and oil, mix to a smooth dough and knead well. Wrap the dough in a damp cloth and set aside for about 30 minutes.

To make the filling, mix together the ricotta cheese and the Parmesan cheese, egg, egg yolk, lemon rind and herbs. Season with salt to taste. Roll the mixture into balls about the size of a walnut, and place on a floured surface until required.

Knead the dough lightly and roll it out into sheets 2 mm/$\frac{1}{16}$in thick. Using a 6-cm/2½-in floured cutter, cut out circles of dough. Alternatively, cut the dough into 6-cm/2½-in squares, using a floured, sharp knife. Place one ball of filling in the centre of each piece of dough. Fold in half and firmly press the edges together, to form a *cappelletto*.

Press the leftover dough into a ball and repeat the process until all the pasta and filling are used up. Bring the broth to the boil and place a few *cappelletti* at a time in a large saucepan half-filled with lightly salted, boiling water. Simmer for 5 to 10 minutes or until they rise to the surface. Serve immediately in heated soup dishes with the cheese.

LASAGNE WITH BOLOGNESE AND CHICKEN SAUCE

SERVES 6

This dish of pasta, layered with poultry, meat sauce and cheese, makes a particularly sustaining dish.

For the pasta
5 eggs
1 teaspoon olive oil
450g/1 lb plain flour
pinch of salt
For the sauce
25g/1 oz butter
175g/6 oz coarsely chopped, cooked chicken
pinch of salt
1 quantity Bolognese sauce (page 56)
40g/1½ oz melted butter
175g/6 oz Parmesan cheese, grated

To make the pasta, lightly whisk the eggs and olive oil in a small bowl. Sift the flour and salt onto a

From Emilia-Romagna: *Bolognese Sauce (overleaf)*

marble slab or into a mixing bowl and make a well in the centre. Pour in the egg and oil mixture, mix to a smooth dough and knead well. Wrap the dough in a damp cloth and set it aside for 30 minutes. Roll the dough into 3 sheets, 2 mm/$\frac{1}{16}$in thick. Cut it into 7.5-cm/3-in squares and cook a few at a time, in a large saucepan half-filled with lightly salted, boiling water for 3 to 5 minutes, or until *al dente* (cooked but still firm). Remove with a perforated spoon, drain well, and cool on a damp cloth.

To make the sauce, heat the butter in a frying pan over a moderate heat. Add the chicken and sauté for 2 to 3 minutes. Season with salt and add the Bolognese sauce.

Pour half the melted butter into an ovenproof dish, add the pasta in layers, covering each layer with a little of the sauce and sprinkling of cheese. Sprinkle the top layer with grated cheese and the remaining melted butter. Bake in a preheated, moderate oven (180C, 350F, gas 4) for 40 to 45 minutes and serve with the remaining grated cheese.

BOLOGNESE SAUCE

MAKES 450 ml/¾ pint

(Illustrated on previous page)
This is probably the best known Italian sauce – if it is well made with the very best ingredients, it is a perfect accompaniment to pasta dishes.

25 g/1 oz butter
½ small onion, chopped
½ small carrot, chopped
1 small clove garlic, peeled and chopped
1 small stick celery, chopped
2 tablespoons olive oil
50 g/2 oz ham or lean bacon, chopped
3 dried mushrooms, soaked, drained and chopped, or 3 fresh mushrooms, chopped
225 g/8 oz coarsely minced beef
5 tablespoons dry red wine
sprig parsley
sprig marjoram
salt and pepper
2 teaspoons plain flour
4 tomatoes, peeled and chopped

Heat the butter in a frying pan over a moderate heat, add the onion, carrot, garlic and celery and sauté until lightly browned. Remove the frying pan from the heat and set aside. Heat the olive oil in a saucepan over a moderate heat, add the ham and sauté until lightly browned. Add the onion mixture, mushrooms and beef. Cook for 10 to 15 minutes over a moderate heat, then pour the wine over the ingredients. Chop the parsley and marjoram together, add to the frying pan and season with salt and pepper.

When the wine is reduced to 1 teaspoon, remove the frying pan from the heat and stir in the flour. Mix thoroughly, then return to the heat and cook the mixture very gently for 10 to 15 minutes, stirring constantly. Add the tomatoes and cook, adding 1 tablespoon of water occasionally to prevent the sauce from sticking. Remove the frying pan from the heat as soon as the sauce is well-blended and slightly thickened.

RIBBON NOODLES WITH BOLOGNESE SAUCE

SERVES 6

Italian cooks have devised many utensils for the preparation and shaping of their various pastas. The oldest is the *chittarra*, a wooden frame with guitar-like strings or wires. The dough was rolled over and pressed through the wires, emerging as the flat ribbon noodles. Today, of course, this has been perfected and mechanised.

5 eggs
1 teaspoon olive oil
450 g/1 lb plain flour
1 teaspoon salt
1 quantity Bolognese Sauce (left)
100 g/4 oz butter
100 g/4 oz Reggiano cheese, grated

Lightly whisk together the eggs and olive oil in a small bowl. Sift the flour and salt on to a marble slab or into a mixing bowl and make a well in the centre. Pour in the eggs and oil, mix to a smooth dough and knead well. Wrap the dough in a damp cloth and set it aside for about 30 minutes. Roll the dough into two sheets, 2 mm/$\frac{1}{16}$ in thick. Fold each sheet in half lengthways, then in half again and, with a sharp knife, cut the dough into noodles, 5 mm/$\frac{1}{4}$ in thick. Unroll the noodles immediately and leave them to dry on a lightly floured surface for 10 to 15 minutes.

Place the tagliatelle into a large saucepan, half-filled with lightly salted, boiling water. Simmer for 3 to 5 minutes, or until *al dente* (cooked but still firm).

Remove with a perforated spoon, drain and place on a heated serving plate.

Meanwhile, heat the Bolognese Sauce. Cut the butter into small pieces and place on top of the noodles. Cover with half the cheese and half the meat sauce. Bring to the table, mix, and serve immediately with the remaining cheese and the meat sauce.

From Emilia-Romagna: *Ribbon Noodles with Bolognese Sauce (opposite)*

STUFFED CAPON

SERVES 6

Stracecchio cheese – a three-year-old Parmesan cheese – is traditionally used in this recipe.

*I (about 1.75-kg/4-lb) capon
salt and pepper
100 g/4 oz Parmesan cheese, grated
75 g/3 oz butter
2 eggs
75 g/3 oz fine fresh breadcrumbs
I clove
I small onion
I small carrot
I stick celery*

Using a sharp knife, remove and discard the breast bone from the capon. Season the cavity with salt and pepper. Mix together the cheese, butter, eggs, breadcrumbs and salt and pepper to make a soft stuffing. Fill the bird with the stuffing and sew the opening and truss the bird with fine string.

Place it in a flameproof casserole or a large saucepan and cover with lightly salted cold water. Place over a moderate heat, bring to the boil and skim the surface carefully. Stick the clove into the onion and add with the carrot and the celery to the stock. Reduce the heat, cover tightly and simmer for about 1½ hours or until tender.

Remove the capon, drain it well and remove the string. Carve the capon and place it on a heated serving plate.

SKEWERED VEAL AND SAUSAGE

This recipe and those which follow on pages 58 and 59 are all served together to make the famous Emilian meal of *Fritto Misto Bolognese*. This consists of a selection of individually fried dishes – the more the merrier. Since all the dishes should be ready simultaneously, it is important to prepare those that need the longest cooking first. Combined, the meal consisting of these seven dishes will serve six persons.

*225 g/8 oz fillet of veal or pork
salt and pepper
75 g/3 oz butter
225 g/8 oz mortadella sausage, cubed
100 g/4 oz Parmesan or Gruyère
cheese, cubed
2 thick slices bread, crusts removed
about 150 ml/¼ pint warm milk
about 100 g/4 oz plain flour
I egg, mixed with 2 teaspoons water
100 g/4 oz dried breadcrumbs*

Season the veal or pork with salt and pepper. Heat the butter in a frying pan, add the veal and sauté for about 10 minutes, or until tender. Drain well and set aside to cool.

Cut the meat into 2.5-cm/1-in cubes. Thread the meat, sausage, cheese and bread alternately on to long wooden skewers. Brush the skewered ingredients with the milk and sprinkle with the flour. Beat the egg with the salt, brush the ingredients with the egg mixture and coat with the breadcrumbs. Deep-fry in hot oil until golden brown. Drain well and serve hot.

CHICKEN CROQUETTES

Croquettes are always a popular snack by themselves, but these refined chicken croquettes form an integral part of *fritto misto*.

225 g/8 oz cooked chicken, minced
⅓ quantity White Sauce (page 19)
1 tablespoon grated Parmesan cheese
1 egg
pinch of salt
50 g/2 oz plain flour
100 g/4 oz fine fresh breadcrumbs
oil for deep frying

Mix the minced chicken with the hot white sauce and add the cheese while the mixture is still hot. Spread it out on a plate to cool and shape it into croquettes, about 1-cm × 6-cm/½-in × 2½-in. Beat the egg with the salt and coat each croquette with flour, then dip each into the egg mixture and coat with the breadcrumbs. Deep-fry in hot oil until golden brown. Drain well and serve hot.

FRIED CALF'S LIVER

Calf's liver is easy and quick to prepare. The less expensive lamb's liver may also be used.

2 tablespoons plain flour
¼ teaspoon salt
pinch of pepper
225 g/8 oz calf's liver, thinly sliced
50 g/2 oz butter
2 teaspoons lemon juice
1 teaspoon chopped parsley

Mix the flour with the salt and pepper and coat the liver with the seasoned flour. Melt the butter in a heavy frying pan. Add the liver and sauté for 5 to 6 minutes, or until tender. Serve sprinkled with lemon juice and parsley.

BREADED LAMB CUTLETS

These thin lamb cutlets take only a few minutes to prepare.

4 (about 100 g/4 oz each) lamb cutlets
1 egg
pinch of salt
breadcrumbs
75 g/3 oz butter

Trim the skin and excess fat from the cutlets, and beat them lightly with a meat mallet or wooden rolling pin.
   Beat the egg with the salt and coat the meat with the egg mixture and the breadcrumbs. Melt the butter in a heavy frying pan. Add the cutlets and sauté for 4 to 5 minutes on each side or until tender and golden brown. Drain, and serve hot.

SAUTÉED COURGETTES

No true mixed fry is complete without vegetables and these courgettes give a delightful Mediterranean touch.

1 egg
pinch of salt
225 g/8 oz courgettes, trimmed, cut into quarters lengthways
2 tablespoons plain flour
3 tablespoons olive oil

Beat the egg with the salt and coat the strips of courgette with flour and the egg mixture. Heat the olive oil in a frying pan, add the courgettes and sauté them for 2 to 3 minutes on each side, or until tender and golden brown. Drain well and serve hot.

DEEP-FRIED CAULIFLOWER

The cauliflower may be parboiled beforehand so that the sprigs can be deep-fried in a few minutes, to be ready together with the other components of the meal.

1 (about 450–575 g| 1–1¼ lb)
cauliflower
1 beaten egg
pinch of salt
breadcrumbs for coating
oil for deep frying

Remove the tough stalks from the cauliflower and rinse under cold running water. Simmer lightly in salted boiling water until barely tender. The cauliflower must not be overcooked. Drain well and break into florets.

Beat the egg with the salt and coat the florets with the egg mixture and the breadcrumbs and deep-fry in hot oil for 2 to 3 minutes, or until golden brown. Drain well and serve hot.

DEEP-FRIED ARTICHOKE HEARTS

Artichoke hearts are another typical southern component in a *fritto misto.*

4 large or 8 small artichokes
1 tablespoon lemon juice
2 tablespoons flour
about 150 ml|¼ pint oil

Remove and discard the leaves and choke from each artichoke, leaving only the heart. Cut into quarters and place in a bowl. Cover with water and add the lemon juice. Set aside for 1 to 2 hours.

Drain the hearts well on kitchen paper and coat them with the flour. Deep-fry them in hot oil for 2 to 3 minutes, or until golden brown. Drain well and serve hot.

From Emilia-Romagna: *Fritto Misto Bolognese (see note page 57)*

Tuscany

Florence, city of the Medicis, Machiavelli, Boccaccio, Michelangelo, Giotto, and Dante; Sienna, where horses ride in the main square; and Pisa of the leaning tower: these are just some of Tuscany's attractions. But to the wine-bibber, Tuscany is the home of Chianti, best known of all Italian wines.

Chianti, which comes in the characteristic straw-covered flasks, is available in white as well as red varieties. Only when it comes from the region between Florence and Sienna may it bear the official yellow seal that entitles it to be sold as Chianti Classico. Tuscany produces about a hundred million gallons of wine a year, almost all of it very acceptable. Most Tuscan wines are drunk young. If matured for two years, they qualify as vecchio, or old wine. Stravecchio is wine that has been matured for three years or more.

Tuscany is also the home of olive oil, really excellent meat and vegetables, and good plain cooking. Sauces, spices, and herbs play little part in the Tuscan cuisine. Steaks and chickens, mainly of the local breed, are cooked very simply: brushed, perhaps, with olive oil and grilled whole.

A favourite Tuscan snack, which typifies the simplicity of the regional cooking, is bruschetta: slices of white bread baked in the oven until they are crisp and golden, rubbed with garlic, and eaten with the limpid, fruity Tuscan olive oil, not to mention copious draughts of Tuscan wine.

FISH SOUP

SERVES 6

It is said that this soup, known as cacciucco, was invented in Leghorn, the centre of the fishing industry. It is a very rich fish soup that can change according to the whim of the cook, who also believes that the height of perfection is reached by boiling a stone from the sea bed with the fish.

1.5 kg/3 lb mixed white sea fish (sole, perch, red mullet, hake, shrimps, lobster or eel)
6 tablespoons olive oil
2 cloves garlic, chopped
1 small onion, chopped
$\frac{1}{4}$ small chilli, deseeded and chopped
450 g/1 lb tomatoes, peeled and chopped
1 tablespoon chopped parsley
450 ml/$\frac{3}{4}$ pint dry white wine
1 litre/1$\frac{3}{4}$ pints water
salt
6 slices French bread, rubbed with garlic, to serve

Fillet the fish. Clean, wash and trim the shellfish and eel, if used, and cut the flesh into 5-cm/2-in pieces.

Heat the olive oil in a large saucepan over a moderate heat and lightly sauté the garlic, onion and the chilli. Add the tomato, parsley, wine and water and season with salt and bring to the boil, lower the heat and continue cooking for about 30 minutes. Add the fish, the firmest ones first, then the others. Continue cooking over a moderate heat for 15 minutes.

Place a slice of bread in each soup plate, then place a piece of fish on top. Pour the soup over the fish and serve immediately.

GRILLED LIVER

SERVES 6

450 g/1 lb pig's liver
2 cloves garlic
100 g/4 oz dried breadcrumbs
4 thick slices bread, crusts removed
1 egg, beaten
flour for coating
salt and pepper
bay leaves
olive oil
100 g/4 oz Parmesan cheese, grated
1 quantity Risotto (page 24)

Remove and discard any membrane and white fatty parts from the liver. Rinse the liver under cold running water and pat dry with a cloth or kitchen paper. Cut the liver into 3.5-cm/1½-in pieces.

Peel and finely chop the garlic and mix with the breadcrumbs. Cut the bread into large cubes. Stir a little water into the beaten egg.

Coat each piece of liver in a little flour, dip in egg and roll in the breadcrumbs and season. Thread onto long metal skewers, alternating the liver with bay leaves and cubes of bread. Sprinkle with olive oil and cook on a spit over glowing charcoal or cook

From Tuscany: _Hare in Savoury Sauce (page 64)_

under a moderately hot grill for 10 to 15 minutes, or until well browned and tender. Serve immediately with the cheese and risotto.

GRILLED T-BONE STEAKS

SERVES 6

6 T-bone steaks
2 tablespoons olive oil
salt and pepper

Brush both sides of each steak with olive oil and sprinkle with pepper. Set aside to marinate for about 10 minutes. Grill to taste over a charcoal fire or under a hot grill. Season with salt.

PORK WITH CELERY

SERVES 6

1 kg/2 lb loin of pork
$\frac{1}{4}$ teaspoon dried rosemary
$\frac{1}{4}$ teaspoon dried sage
salt and pepper
1 clove garlic
50 g/2 oz butter
2 tablespoons chopped onion
5 tablespoons dry white wine
2 heads celery, chopped
450 g/1 lb tomatoes, peeled and
chopped
50 g/2 oz minced lean and fat ham

Bone the loin of pork and lightly beat it with a meat mallet. Crush the rosemary and sage to a powder. Rub the pork with the herbs, season with salt and pepper and tie into a neat shape with fine string.

Peel and crush the garlic. Heat half the butter in a saucepan over a moderate heat, add the garlic and half the onion and sauté until golden brown. Add the pork and sauté for 5 minutes on each side, or until well browned. Pour in the wine and reduce it to 1 teaspoon, then lower the heat, cover tightly and simmer for 45 minutes. During this time, baste the pork frequently and add 1 tablespoon of hot water if necessary to prevent the pork from sticking.

Meanwhile, trim and wash the celery. Cut into thick slices. Heat the remaining butter in a saucepan over a moderate heat, add the ham and the remaining onion and sauté until lightly browned. Add the tomatoes. Season with salt and pepper and cook for about 20 minutes. Strain the ham mixture through a fine sieve into a second saucepan. Add the celery and simmer over a moderate heat for 10 minutes. Untie the loin of pork, carve it into slices and arrange them on a heated serving dish. Surround them with the celery in the tomato sauce and serve immediately.

DEVILLED CHICKEN

SERVES 6

In Tuscany, chickens are small, plump and tender. Charcoal or wood is normally used for cooking. If the chicken is placed under a grill, reduce the cooking time by 10 minutes.

1 (2-kg/4-lb) chicken
150 ml/$\frac{1}{4}$ pint olive oil
few sprigs parsley
2–3 rosemary sprigs
salt and pepper
1 clove garlic, crushed
juice of 1 lemon

Split the chicken along the back-bone but do not cut it completely in half. Lightly beat it with a meat mallet or wooden rolling pin so that it remains flat. Remove and discard as many bones as possible.

Place the chicken in a bowl with the olive oil, parsley, rosemary and salt and pepper. Add the garlic and lemon juice to the chicken and set aside to marinate for 1 hour.

Cook the chicken over the hot embers of a charcoal fire until it is golden brown on each side. Move the chicken further away from the source of heat and cook for a further 40 to 45 minutes, or until tender. During the cooking, turn the chicken frequently and brush it with the marinade.

From Umbria: *Spaghetti with Cheese and Bacon* (page 66)

HARE IN SAVOURY SAUCE

SERVES 6

(Illustrated on page 61)

1 (1.5-kg/3-lb) hare, jointed
½ small onion, sliced
½ stick celery, sliced
1 bay leaf, crumbled
450 ml/¾ pint full-bodied red wine
2 peppercorns
For the pasta
4 eggs
1 tablespoon olive oil
450 g/1 lb plain flour
pinch of salt
For the sauce
1 tablespoon olive oil
½ onion, chopped
½ carrot, chopped
2 rashers rindless bacon, chopped
pinch of ground nutmeg
chicken stock
50 g/2 oz butter

To make the marinade, place the onion, celery and bay leaf in a bowl with the wine and peppercorns. Add the hare and marinate for several hours.

To make the pasta, lightly whisk together the eggs and olive oil in a small bowl. Sift the flour and salt on to a marble slab or into a mixing bowl and make a well in the centre. Pour in the eggs and the oil, mix to a firm, smooth dough and knead well. Wrap in a damp cloth, set aside for 30 minutes. Roll the dough on a floured surface to about 2 mm/1/16 in thick. With a sharp knife, cut the dough into noodles, about 5 mm/¼ in wide. Set aside on a floured surface to dry until required.

To make the sauce, heat the oil in a frying pan over a moderate heat, add the onion, carrot and bacon and sauté until lightly browned. Drain the pieces of hare, season with salt and the nutmeg, place in the frying pan and sauté until browned Lower the heat and cook gently for about 1¼–1½ hours or until tender, occasionally adding 1 tablespoon of the marinade and 1 tablespoon of the stock to form a thin sauce. Remove the hare, strain the sauce and replace the meat. Keep hot.

Cook the noodles in lightly salted, boiling water for 8 to 12 minutes. Drain, and serve dotted with butter. Lightly sautéed courgettes are also a good accompaniment for the hare.

MEAT SAUCE

MAKES 600 ml/1 pint

100 g/4 oz pork or ham rind
100 g/4 oz lean bacon in 1 piece
450 g/1 lb beef topside
2 teaspoons salt
¼ teaspoon pepper
40 g/1½ oz ham or gammon, finely chopped or minced
2 medium-sized carrots, sliced
1 medium-sized onion, sliced
1 clove garlic, chopped
1 stick celery, chopped
3 dried mushrooms, soaked, drained and chopped or 3 fresh mushrooms, sliced
1 clove
bouquet garni (bay leaf, sprig of thyme, sprig of marjoram)
4 tablespoons dry red wine
25 g/1 oz plain flour
1 large tomato, peeled and chopped
300 ml/½ pint water

Simmer the pork rind in boiling water for 5 minutes. Drain well and chop coarsely. Cut the bacon into 1-cm/½-in cubes. Make small incisions in the beef and press a cube of bacon into each incision. Sprinkle the beef with the salt and pepper.

Place the pork rind and ham in an ovenproof casserole and sauté them very gently over a low heat until the fat on the rind begins to melt. Place the beef in the casserole with the carrots, onion, garlic, celery, mushrooms and clove. Increase the heat to moderate and sauté the ingredients until the beef begins to brown. Add the bouquet garni and the wine. Increase the heat to high and boil rapidly until the wine is reduced to 1 teaspoon.

Remove the saucepan from the heat and stir in the flour. Return to a moderate heat and simmer for 2 to 3 minutes, stirring constantly. Stir in the tomato and the water. Bring to the boil, remove the saucepan from the heat, cover tightly and cook in a cool oven (150C, 300F, gas 2) for 4 hours.

Remove the beef from the casserole and use in another dish. Press the sauce through a sieve into a saucepan. Place over a moderate heat and simmer gently until it is reduced to a consistency thick enough to coat the back of a spoon. Adjust the seasoning and skim the surface to remove any fat. Pour the sauce into a bowl and set aside to cool. Use as required. This meat sauce will keep for several days in the refrigerator or a cold place.

CRISP FLORENTINE PASTRIES

SERVES 6

These fried Tuscan pastries can be served alone or with a cold dessert, and together with other small pastries were often sold from stalls and barrows at country fairs and markets. Vanilla sugar can be made at home by leaving a vanilla bean in a tightly closed jar of sugar for at least 3 days.

350 g/12 oz plain flour
50 g/2 oz butter
3 eggs
pinch of sugar
pinch of salt
about 300 ml/½ pint oil for deep-frying
about 225 g/8 oz vanilla sugar

Sift the flour onto a marble or wooden surface or into a mixing bowl and make a well in the centre. Place the butter, eggs, sugar and the salt in the well and mix to a dough. Knead until the dough is smooth and firm. Wrap it in a lightly floured cloth and set aside in a cool place for about 1 hour.

Place the dough on a floured surface and cut it into two or three pieces. Roll each piece into a sheet, about 3 mm/⅛ in thick and cut it into circles, rectangles, strips or whatever shapes you prefer.

Heat the oil and fry the pastries, a few at a time, until they are golden brown. Drain well and sprinkle with vanilla sugar. Serve warm or cold.

From Tuscany: *Crisp Florentine Pastries*

Marche to Latium

This is a large area which includes the regions of Umbria and Abruzzi. These are four small provinces which are strung across the middle of Italy, from the Adriatic in the east to Rome in the west. Apart from Latium, which is home of Rome and the Vatican City, this is an area which is sparsely populated.

Umbria is noted for its chocolate and macaroons made from pine nut kernels. Orvieto, Umbria's notable white wine, is not unlike a white Chianti. It is available from dry through to sweet but it travels badly! Other good regional wines include Trasimeno and the strong red Torgiano.

Marche is a mountainous eastern region which offers lots of fish dishes, baked ravioli and polenta. The wines of this area are pleasant, cheap and quite unpretentious.

Abruzzi, south of Marche, is hilly rather than mountainous, with an agricultural and pastoral economy. Potatoes, wheat, grapes, olives and mutton are important products here, along with fish from the Adriatic. Baked pasta dishes and rich chocolate cake for dessert are just a couple of examples of the sort of food to expect of the area.

Probably the most famous wine from the region is Frascati, but Grotta ferrata, full and mellow, is often thought to be better.

SPAGHETTI WITH CHEESE AND BACON

SERVES 6

(Illustrated on page 63)

575 g/ 1¼ lb spaghetti
225 g/ 8 oz rindless bacon rashers
2 tablespoons olive oil
25 g/ 1 oz lard
¼ chilli, deseeded
1 small onion, chopped
1 clove garlic, peeled and chopped
pinch of salt
100 g/ 4 oz Pecorino cheese, grated

Cook the spaghetti in plenty of boiling salted water for about 10 to 12 minutes. Drain, turn into a serving dish and keep hot. Chop the bacon.

Heat the olive oil and lard in a frying pan. Add and brown the bacon and chilli. Remove and set aside. Add the onion, garlic and salt to the pan, stir until lightly browned. Discard the chilli and add the bacon, then sprinkle over the spaghetti with the cheese. Serve at once.

SPAGHETTI WITH PEPPERED CHEESE

SERVES 6

Since this dish could be rather dry with only grated cheese and pepper, a little of the water in which the spaghetti was cooked is usually used to moisten it.

575 g/ 1¼ lb spaghetti
100 g/ 4 oz Cacio cheese, grated
2 teaspoons crushed peppercorns

Cook the spaghetti in plenty of boiling salted water for about 10 to 12 minutes or until al dente (cooked but still firm). Drain it, reserving a little of the cooking liquid.

Place the spaghetti in a large heated serving plate and sprinkle with the cheese and the peppercorns. Sprinkle the surface with a few tablespoons of the cooking water to help melt and blend the cheese. Mix and serve immediately.

ANCHOVY OMELETTE

SERVES 6

A savoury omelette in the Italian style. The anchovies are an integral part of the omelette which is cooked on both sides and served flat.

*1 (50-g/2-oz) can anchovy fillets,
drained
3 tablespoons milk
1 tablespoon chopped parsley
3 generous tablespoons olive oil
1 clove garlic, peeled and crushed
350 g/12 oz tomatoes, peeled and
chopped
1 small chilli
salt
10 eggs
pepper*

Soak the anchovies in the milk for about 10 minutes to remove the excess salt. Drain and pound to a paste with the parsley.

Heat one-third of the olive oil in a frying pan over a moderate heat, add the garlic and sauté until

From Umbria: *Pasta with Mushroom, Chilli and Tomato Sauce (overleaf)*

lightly browned. Discard the garlic and add the anchovy mixture to the pan, then add the tomatoes and the chilli and season with a little salt. Continue cooking for 8 minutes, then pour the mixture into a bowl and let stand until cool. Discard the chilli, beat the eggs well and stir into the cooled anchovy mixture, then season with salt and pepper.

Heat half the remaining oil in the frying pan over a moderate heat and pour in the egg mixture. Stir the upper portion of the mixture for a few seconds until the bottom of the omelette is golden brown. Continue cooking for 1 to 2 minutes until the mixture begins to set.

Remove the frying pan from the heat and invert the omelette onto a large, round plate. Heat the remaining oil in the frying pan and slide the omelette into the frying pan with the browned side up. Cook until golden brown, then slide onto a round, heated serving plate and serve immediately.

PASTA WITH MUSHROOM, CHILLI AND TOMATO SAUCE

SERVES 6

(Illustrated on previous page)

According to this and several other recipes, the garlic and chilli pepper are used only to flavour the oil and are then discarded. However, this appears not to happen in an Italian trattoria; in fact, extra garlic and chilli are often provided!

175 g/6 oz very lean, rindless rashers bacon
350 g/12 oz mushrooms
450 g/1 lb tomatoes
2 cloves garlic
50 g/2 oz butter
½ chilli
few leaves fresh basil, chopped
salt
For the pasta
450 g/1 lb penne or macaroni
50 g/2 oz Parmesan cheese, grated
50 g/2 oz Pecorino cheese, grated
50 g/2 oz butter

Chop the bacon. Wash, dry, and slice the mushrooms. Peel and chop the tomatoes. Peel and slice the garlic. Heat the butter in a frying pan, add the bacon, and sauté until lightly browned. Remove the bacon, drain, set aside, and keep hot. Sauté the mushrooms in the butter remaining in the pan. Remove, drain, and set aside with the bacon. Sauté the garlic and the whole chilli in the remaining fat over moderate heat. When the garlic is golden brown discard it and the chilli pepper. Add the tomatoes to the pan. Sprinkle in the basil and season with salt, then simmer for 20 minutes. Stir the bacon and mushrooms into the tomatoes and simmer gently while cooking the pasta.

Cook the pasta in a large saucepan of lightly salted boiling water. Simmer for 10–15 minutes, until *al dente* (cooked but still firm). Drain and place in a heated deep serving dish. Mix the Parmesan and Pecorino cheeses together and sprinkle over the pasta. Dot with pieces of the butter and pour the sauce over the top. Mix quickly together just before serving.

FRIED FISH ITALIAN STYLE

SERVES 12

This fish dish is one of the most frequently found in restaurant menus along Italy's long coastline. The simple preparation and cooking of the fish allows the diner to appreciate the full flavour of good quality fish.

4 tablespoons olive oil
2.75 kg/6 lb mixed fish, dressed (sole, perch, red mullet, hake or eel)
salt
2 tablespoons lemon juice (optional)

Heat the olive oil in a frying pan over a moderate heat. Add the fish, without drying or flouring them. When cooked, drain and sprinkle generously with salt and the lemon juice, if used. Place on a large serving plate and serve immediately.

FRESH PEAS WITH HAM

SERVES 12

The green peas which are grown around Rome are renowned for their sweetness. They are often cooked with ham, as a vegetable dish or as a sauce for pasta.

5 tablespoons olive oil
½ small onion, finely chopped
1.5 kg/3 lb fresh peas, shelled
pinch of caster sugar
salt and pepper
3–4 tablespoons vegetable stock or water
175 g/6 oz Parma or Bayonne ham, diced
fried croûtons to serve

Heat the olive oil in a frying pan over a moderate heat, add the onion and sauté until lightly browned. Add the peas, season with the sugar and salt and pepper, then pour in the stock.

Simmer gently for 10 minutes. Add the ham. Discard any excess liquid and serve in a heated vegetable dish, surrounded with freshly fried croûtons.

SEAFOOD RISOTTO

SERVES 6

Seafood risotto is a typical Italian dish. Lobster or prawns, or a mixture of both, may be substituted for the scampi, but it is important to have a mixture of different crustaceans for a really authentic dish.

450 ml/¾ pint cockles
450 ml/¾ pint clams or
1 (415-g/14½-oz) can clams, drained
600 ml/1 pint mussels
3 tablespoons dry white wine
5 tablespoons olive oil
1 medium-sized onion, finely chopped
450 g/1 lb Italian rice (or other long-grain rice
1 litre/1¾ pints boiling water
100 g/4 oz peeled scampi, chopped
salt and pepper
1 tablespoon chopped parsley

Thoroughly scrub the shellfish, discarding any which are open and do not shut. Remove the beards from the mussels.

Heat the wine in a saucepan over a high heat, add the cockles, clams and mussels and shake the saucepan over the heat until they open.

Pour them into a colander with a bowl underneath to catch the cooking liquid. Discard any unopened shellfish. Remove the flesh from the shells and reserve.

Heat the olive oil in a large saucepan over a moderate heat, add the onion and sauté until lightly browned. Strain the cooking liquid, add and reduce by half. Add the rice, pour in the boiling water and stir. After about 10 minutes, mix in the cockles, clams, mussels and scampi. Season with salt and a little pepper. Continue cooking over a high heat, occasionally adding 1 tablespoon of boiling water as the rice thickens and dries out. When the rice is *al dente* (cooked but still firm), add the parsley and pour into a deep, heated serving dish. Serve immediately.

From Umbria: *Veal with Ham and Sage in White Wine (overleaf)*

STEWED OXTAIL IN WINE SAUCE

SERVES 6

Oxtail is economical and well flavoured but it needs long cooking if it is to be tender. If the tail is very fatty, the dish may be prepared the day before it is required, up to the point before the celery is added, and left to cool so the fat rises to the top. The next day, remove the fat and complete the dish.

1.5–1.75 kg/3–4 lb oxtail, cut into
5-cm/2-in pieces
1 small carrot
1 leek
3 litres/5 pints cold water
2–3 teaspoons coarse salt
1 small bay leaf
1 small onion
1 kg/2 lb tomatoes
100 g/4 oz gammon
2 tablespoons olive oil
½ teaspoon chopped fresh marjoram,
or ¼ teaspoon dried marjoram
generous 150 ml/¼ pint dry white
wine
pinch of ground nutmeg
salt and pepper
6 celery hearts
pinch of ground cinnamon
1 tablespoon pine kernels
1 tablespoon sultanas

Soak the oxtail for 4 hours in cold water. Place in a large saucepan with plenty of cold water and bring to the boil. Simmer for about 10 minutes, drain well, and dry with a cloth or kitchen paper. Peel the carrot. Trim the leek and wash thoroughly. Return the oxtail to the saucepan then add the measured cold water and the salt. Place over high heat and bring to the boil. Lower the heat and skim carefully. Add the carrot, leek and bay leaf and simmer gently for 3 hours.

Remove the oxtail, drain, and dry with a cloth or kitchen paper. Discard the vegetables and bay leaf and reserve the stock. Peel and finely chop the onion. Peel and chop the tomatoes and press through a sieve. Mince the gammon. Heat the olive oil in a saucepan over moderate heat, add the gammon, onion, and marjoram, and sauté until lightly browned. Add the oxtail. Simmer for 2 to 3 minutes; then pour in the wine and boil until reduced to 1 tablespoon. Stir in the tomatoes,

season with the nutmeg and salt and pepper, and continue cooking for about 1 hour, or until the meat comes away from the bone. If the sauce begins to thicken too much, add a little of the reserved oxtail stock.

Meanwhile, cook the celery hearts in lightly salted boiling water until barely tender. Drain and add to the oxtail with the cinnamon about 10 minutes before the end of the cooking time. Just before serving, stir in the pine nut kernels and the sultanas. Pour into a deep heated serving dish and serve immediately.

VEAL WITH HAM AND SAGE IN WHITE WINE

SERVES 6

(Illustrated on previous page)
This is one of the most famous of all Italian dishes – *saltimbocca*. It is said the dish originated in Brescia, but that it was adopted by Rome. The sage gives the dish its characteristic flavour. Directly translated the name means 'jump into the mouth' which the veal almost does when superbly cooked!

12 thin veal escalopes
salt and freshly milled black pepper
12 fresh sage leaves
12 thin slices prosciutto ham
about 100 g/4 oz plain flour
100 g/4 oz butter
5 tablespoons dry white wine

Flatten the veal with a meat mallet or a wooden rolling pin. Season with the salt and pepper, then place 1 sage leaf and 1 slice of ham on each piece of veal. Roll up the veal or fold in half and secure with a wooden cocktail stick. Coat it lightly with flour.

Heat three-quarters of the butter in a frying pan over a moderate heat and fry the veal until evenly browned and tender. Remove the cocktail sticks, place the veal on a heated serving plate and keep hot.

Pour the wine into the frying pan and reduce it to 1 tablespoon over a high heat. Scrape and stir the bottom of the pan, stir in the remaining butter, simmer for a few seconds, then pour over the *saltimbocca* and serve immediately.

CHICKEN STEW WITH VINEGAR

SERVES 6

In Italian cuisine anchovies are frequently pounded and used as a seasoning, rather than as a predominant flavour or an accompaniment.

*1 (about 1.5-kg/3-lb) chicken, cut into
serving pieces
about 100 g/4 oz plain flour
4 anchovy fillets
2 tablespoons milk or water
(optional)
3 cloves garlic, peeled and chopped
5 tablespoons vinegar
2 tablespoons olive oil
4 sprigs rosemary
salt and pepper
4 tablespoons olive oil
350 g/12 oz potatoes, peeled and
diced*

Coat the chicken lightly with flour. Soak the anchovy fillets in the milk for 15 minutes to remove the excess salt. Drain them and pound them to a

From Umbria: *Chicken Stew with Vinegar*

paste with the garlic. Stir in the vinegar. Heat the olive oil in a frying pan over a moderate heat. Tie 3 sprigs of the rosemary together and add them with the chicken to the pan. Brown the chicken evenly. Remove it from the pan and season with salt and pepper. Discard the rosemary.

Add the garlic mixture to the liquid remaining in the frying pan. Reduce the liquid by two-thirds over high heat. Return the chicken to the frying pan and simmer it for about 15 to 20 minutes, or until tender, stirring frequently.

Place the olive oil in a second frying pan, add the potatoes and the remaining sprig of rosemary and sauté until tender. Drain the potatoes and season them with salt and pepper. Serve the chicken in a heated dish together with the potatoes.

SPAGHETTI WITH EGG AND CHEESE

SERVES 6

This is the well known Spaghetti alla Carbonara.

450 g/ 1 lb spaghetti
1 tablespoon olive oil
6 rindless rashers lean bacon, cut into strips
50 g/2 oz Pecorino cheese, grated
pinch of salt and pepper
6 eggs, beaten
3–4 tablespoons single cream (optional)
50 g/2 oz butter

Cook the spaghetti in plenty of salted boiling water for 10 to 12 minutes, or until *al dente* (cooked but still firm). Drain well. Heat the olive oil in a frying pan, add the bacon, and sauté until brown. Remove and set aside. Stir the cheese, salt and pepper and cream (if used) into the eggs.

Melt the butter in a large saucepan and cook until lightly browned. Pour in the egg mixture, cook gently, stirring until very slightly thickened. Add the spaghetti and the bacon. Remove the saucepan from the heat, mix well, and serve.

BEANS WITH BACON

SERVES 6

The exceptionally good flavour of vegetables such as peas, beans, artichokes, and lettuce grown in this region is said to be due to the mineral content of the volcanic soil.

350 g/ 12 oz dried haricot beans
1 meaty ham bone
1 sprig fresh or dried rosemary
175 g/6 oz fat streaky bacon in one piece
¼ onion
½ clove garlic
350 g/ 12 oz tomatoes
1 tablespoon olive oil
1 tablespoon chopped parsley
salt and freshly milled black pepper

Soak the beans overnight in plenty of cold water. Place the ham bone in a large saucepan half filled with boiling water and simmer for 10 minutes. Carefully drain the ham bone, put in a saucepan and cover with cold water. Drain the beans, add to the ham bone with the rosemary, and simmer for 45 to 50 minutes, or until tender. Remove the ham bone and beans and reserve the cooking liquid.

Simmer the bacon for 2 to 3 minutes in boiling water, then drain and cut into finger-sized pieces. Peel and chop the onion and garlic. Peel the tomatoes and press through a sieve. Heat the olive oil in a second small pan, add the onion, garlic, bacon fingers and parsley, and sauté until lightly browned. Add the tomatoes, season with salt and pepper, and continue cooking over moderate heat for 20 minutes.

Place the beans in a flameproof casserole or a saucepan. Add the tomato mixture. Cut all the meat from the ham bone, dice it and add to the beans. Place the casserole over moderate heat and simmer for 20 to 30 minutes. If the sauce thickens too much, dilute it with a few tablespoons of the reserved cooking liquid or hot water. Serve as hot as possible, straight from the casserole.

STUFFED TOMATOES

SERVES 6

Italian tomatoes are large, juicy and succulent with a sweet flavour, since they are sun-ripened. Where Italian tomatoes are available, it is preferred to serve one very large tomato per person, rather than two medium-sized ones.

12 firm, medium-sized tomatoes
2 cloves garlic, peeled and chopped
small bunch fresh mint
175 g/6 oz Italian rice (or other long-gran rice)
3 tablespoons olive oil
¼ teaspoon salt
pinch of freshly milled black pepper
150 ml/¼ pint water
1 tablespoon concentrated tomato purée

Remove the top from each tomato to form a lid. Remove the pulp and press it through a fine sieve.

Reserve the pulp, discarding the seeds remaining in the sieve. Pound the garlic to a pulp together with the mint.

Place the rice in a bowl with the tomato pulp, garlic mixture, 2 tablespoons of the olive oil and the salt and pepper. Blend together thoroughly.

Place the tomatoes in a greased casserole and sprinkle with a half of the remaining olive oil and salt. Fill each tomato two-thirds full of the rice mixture, then cover it with the tomato lid.

Mix the water into the tomato purée and pour it into the casserole. It should reach halfway up the sides of the tomatoes. Sprinkle the tomatoes with the remaining oil and salt and place in a hot oven (220C, 425F, gas 7). Cook for 40 minutes, or until tender. These are excellent served either hot or cold.

From Umbria: *Stuffed Tomatoes*

St. Joseph's Sugar Puffs

SERVES 6

St. Joseph's Day is celebrated in Italy with much feasting, since he is patron saint of hearth and home. This is one of the many dishes which have become specialities for this saint's day.

75 g/3 oz butter
pinch of salt
300 ml/½ pint cold water
175 g/6 oz plain flour
4 eggs
2 egg yolks
1 teaspoon sugar
2 teaspoons grated lemon rind
150 ml/¼ pint olive oil
100 g/4 oz lard
about 100 g/4 oz vanilla sugar

Place the butter and salt in a saucepan and add the water. Place over a low heat and bring to the boil. Remove from the heat and add the flour all at once. Blend together thoroughly with a wooden spoon, then replace over the heat and stir until the paste

From Umbria: *Trifle (opposite)*

comes away from the sides of the pan to form a ball. When it begins to sizzle, remove the pan from the heat, allow it to cool very slightly, then beat in the eggs and the yolks one at a time, beating thoroughly after each addition. When tiny bubbles appear, add the sugar and the lemon rind and mix until thoroughly blended. Form into a ball, remove from the pan and wrap in a cloth. Leave in a cool place for about 30 minutes.

Shape the dough into walnut-sized balls. Heat the olive oil and lard in a large saucepan over a moderate heat, and drop in several of the balls. The sugar puffs will turn over automatically in the hot oil. When they begin to swell, increase the heat. Fry for about 5 to 10 minutes, or until golden brown, then remove and drain them.

Let the oil cool slightly, then repeat the procedure with several more balls. It is best to fry only a few sugar puffs at a time. Arrange them on a serving dish covered with a doily and sprinkle them with vanilla sugar. Serve very hot.

TRIFLE

SERVES 6

This rich dessert was a gift from the Neapolitans to Lord Nelson after his 1798 victory over Napoleon. 'English soup', as it was called, was the creation of an anonymous pastry cook, smitten with the admiral and the English and their spirit-soaked trifles. Alkermes is a liqueur flavoured with cinnamon, cloves and other spices.

1 (20-cm/8-in) sponge cake
3 tablespoons Alkermes liqueur or
other fruit-flavoured liqueur
3 tablespoons rum
1 tablespoon cold water
For the custard
450 ml/¾ pint milk
175 g/7 oz caster sugar
50 g/2 oz plain flour
3 egg yolks
1 tablespoon finely chopped mixed
candied peel
For the meringue
3 egg whites
strips candied orange peel
caster sugar

Cut the sponge cake horizontally in half and place the slices on two plates. Sprinkle the liqueur over the cake on one plate. Dilute the rum with the water and sprinkle it over the other cake. Set aside for 20 to 30 minutes.

To make the custard, scald the milk in a small saucepan. Mix 75 g/3 oz of the sugar and the flour together in a second saucepan. Lightly beat the egg yolks and blend them into the sugar mixture. Gradually stir in the hot milk. Place over a low heat and cook for about 5 minutes or until the mixture thickens, stirring constantly with a wooden spoon or whisk, until it has a thick pouring consistency.

Spread 3 tablespoons of the custard in a round ovenproof serving dish, about 30 cm/12 in. in diameter. Arrange the cake soaked in liqueur on top. Add the candied peel to the remaining custard, stir, then spoon over the cake. Arrange the sponge slices soaked in rum on top in a dome shape.

To make the meringue, beat the egg whites until stiff and fold in the rest of the sugar. Spread the meringue smoothly over the surface of the trifle with a palette knife or spatula. Decorate with the orange peel and lightly sprinkle with sugar. Place in a preheated moderate oven (160C, 325F, gas 3) for about 30 minutes or until the meringue is very lightly browned. Set aside to cool.

RICOTTA PIE

SERVES 6

For the pastry
350 g/12 oz plain flour
175 g/6 oz caster sugar
75 g/3 oz lard, cut into small pieces
75 g/3 oz butter, chilled, cut into
small pieces
1 egg
2 egg yolks
1 egg, beaten with 1 tablespoon
water
For the filling
575 g/1¼ lb ricotta cheese
225 g/8 oz caster sugar
½ teaspoon grated lemon rind
1 teaspoon grated orange rind
pinch of ground cinnamon
1 egg
3 egg yolks
1 tablespoon brandy
50 g/2 oz sultanas
40 g/1½ oz pine kernels
25 g/1 oz mixed candied peel,
chopped
4 tablespoons vanilla sugar

To make the pastry, sift the flour and sugar on to a marble slab or into a mixing bowl, make a well in the centre and add the lard, butter, egg and egg yolks. With the fingertips, gradually mix the ingredients to a firm dough. Knead lightly until smooth. Cover, set aside for 30 minutes.

To make the filling, place the cheese, sugar, lemon and orange rind and cinnamon in a mixing bowl. Add the egg, egg yolks and brandy and mix well. Stir in the sultanas, pine kernels and the candied peel.

Roll the pastry into 2 fairly thin sheets, the first slightly larger than the second. Sprinkle the surface with a little flour. Line a 25-cm/10-in greased round flan tin or dish with the larger sheet.

Spread the filling evenly in the pastry. Cut the second sheet of pastry into thin strips and weave them in a lattice pattern over the filling. Roll out the leftover dough and make a border for the pie. Brush the pie with the egg-and-water mixture.

Place the pie in a preheated moderate oven (180C, 350F, gas 4) and bake for about 30 minutes, or until golden brown. Remove it from the oven and leave it to cool slightly. Sprinkle with vanilla sugar and serve warm or cold.

Index